Welcome to Happy Valley – where the
skies are always blue, with maybe just a cloud
or two – and apple-cheeked children play outside every day
with chickens, puppies, and red wagons with wooden sides. Driving
down Main Street, you're apt to see a quilt or two hung out over a fence to dry
or a clothesline dangling "Flying Geese" next to a pair of Granddaddy's long johns!

Table of Contents

Quilt to your heart's delight...
Then savor a tasty bite!

EDITORIAL STAFF

Vice President and Editor-in-Chief:
Sandra Graham Case
Executive Director of Publications:
Cheryl Nodine Gunnells
Senior Publications Director:
Susan White Sullivan
Publications Operations Director:
Cheryl Johnson
Editorial Director: Susan Frantz Wiles
Photography Director: Stephen Wilson
Photography Supervisor: Karen Hall
Art Operations Director: Jeff Curtis
TECHNICAL
Technical Editor: Lisa Lancaster
Technical Writer: Frances Huddleston
EDITORIAL
Senior Editor: Steven M. Cooper
Associate Editor: Susan McManus Johnson
ART
Art Publications Director: Rhonda Shelby
Art Imaging Director: Mark Hawkins
Art Category Manager: Lora Puls
Graphic Artists: Amy Gerke, Stephanie
Hamling, and Brittany Skarda
Illustrator: Cherece Athy
Photostylists: Sondra Daniel,
Janna Laughlin, and Cassie Newsome
Staff Photographer: Russell Ganser
Publishing Systems Administrator:
Becky Riddle
Publishing Systems Assistants:
Clint Hanson, John Rose,
and Chris Wertenberger
FOODS
Foods Editor: Celia Fahr Harkey, R.D.

The lively, likable residents of Happy Valley portrayed in this book are the creation of Nan Slaughter, a Seattle quilt designer. Leisure Arts asked Nan to tell us more about her quilts, recipes, and fiction.

Is Happy Valley a real place?

"Yes! The Happy Valley Quilters are all imaginary, but Happy Valley is a real community that's just a short drive from my house. I get in my car and go there often. In fact, that's how I want to share my fictional version of Happy Valley — I want readers to feel that they're riding in my car with me, and I'm pointing out each of the Happy Valley landmarks. And as we drive along, I'm telling them about Eudora, Mae, Merle, Ginny, Beverly, Inga, Emma, and Alice."

Which came first, the quilts or the Happy Valley Quilters?

"When I decided to publish my patterns, I was a little insecure about putting my designs out there for everyone to see. So I looked at each quilt and asked myself 'what kind of person would make this?' The characters claimed their quilts, so it was easier for me to step back and say 'this is Eudora's French quilt,' or 'that one hangs in Mae's living room.'"

What's your favorite part of the story?

"What I love about Happy Valley is that it's a place that's frozen in time. In my version, there may be upsets and a few surprises, but the people pull together and get on with life. And the Happy Valley in my story could be anywhere. It could be in the South, where Eudora's Grits Soufflé might be a common dish, or it could be in the North, hence the Maple Syrup Sauce."

Did you develop the recipes just for the story?

"The recipes are my own family's favorites. Mae's Lettuce Wraps, for example, came about when I was trying one of those low carbohydrate diets. I couldn't use bread for a BLT sandwich, so I wrapped the bacon and tomato in the lettuce. And we always have Funeral Potatoes in the freezer, ready for any occasion."

How long have you been a quilter?

"At least twenty-five years. I have two children, and they argue over the quilts, even though they already have several. I think that's because quilts are such a personal thing — all filled up with memories — that it's hard to imagine not having them. I love that quilts tell a story, and that two pieces of fabric can become one person's work of art. Quilts are just such a part of our lives."

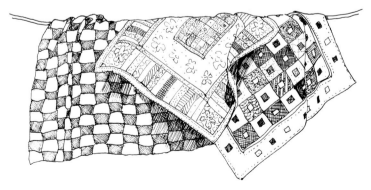

The Quilters of

Merle

Happy Valley

Take a minute to breathe in slowly... you'll discover the wonderful aroma of Merle's Green Apple Pie, fresh from the oven and set out to cool.

She never worries about crows or other critters getting into her baked goods because Old Earl made her a wire "bake-cage" to keep everything safe until he can set himself down to cut the first piece. Merle bakes every day, starts out with buns in the morning, and a pie by noontime.

Late in the day she'll have Maury or Oprah on the TV while she throws together one of her famous casseroles. She calls them all "KFC's." That stands for kitchen/fridge casserole — she just uses whatever is available in her kitchen/fridge that day and they always taste great. Merle's secret ingredient is fennel - grows it herself in the yard and it generally shows up in almost everything she makes.

After dinner Merle can be found propped in the Lazy Boy working on a quilt or a piece of appliqué, which is her specialty. She gets her ideas from everywhere, too, even her dining room wallpaper pattern worked its way into a quilt. Merle is the valley's best quilter - just ask her, she'll tell you!

Eudora

Towards the middle of town is the Happy Valley Grange Hall, where most of the socializing is done.

You won't get two feet inside the front hall before you feast your eyes on Eudora's first place entry in the County Fair's Quilt category. She's 82 years old and has been quilting for just 5 years! Before that, she was too busy flying the crop duster for the valley and raising 11 kids, 56 grandkids and 7 great-grandkids! She's buried three husbands, and is currently courting the future fourth "Mr. Eudora." When the rheumatoid forced her to ground the plane, she finally decided to take up an indoor sport...quilting. She calls it a sport because she has to wear so much paraphernalia just to be able to take a stitch or two. 'Cause of her arthritis and all, she's got to wear these stretchy gloves for circulation. Then since her eyesight has gotten worse, she wears an old miner's light on her head to help her see. Eudora has always been a little bent over because she's so big busted, so now to help her so she doesn't fall face forward when she quilts she straps herself into this arching contraption that her son made for her. By the time she's ready to thread the needle, a half an hour has passed and it's time for a potty break! Somehow she has managed to start and finish 32 quilts in the last 5 years - she's a winner all right!

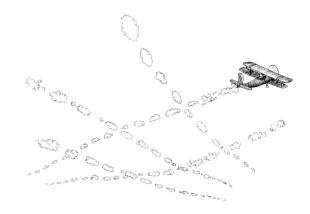

The Grange Hall has a permanent exhibit of the Happy Valley Quilters' quilts hanging on the walls. Eudora is the Happy Valley Quilters' President. She founded the group by inviting every able-bodied woman over 60 with an IQ of room temperature or above to come to her house for a quilting lesson and some of her famous cheese-grits pie. Wouldn't you know that everyone she invited came — everyone except Alice, but I'll get to her later. Merle gave the demonstration, since she's been quilting for nearly half a century. Everyone was duly impressed and decided right then and there that they would join the club. Thus the Happy Valley Quilters were born!

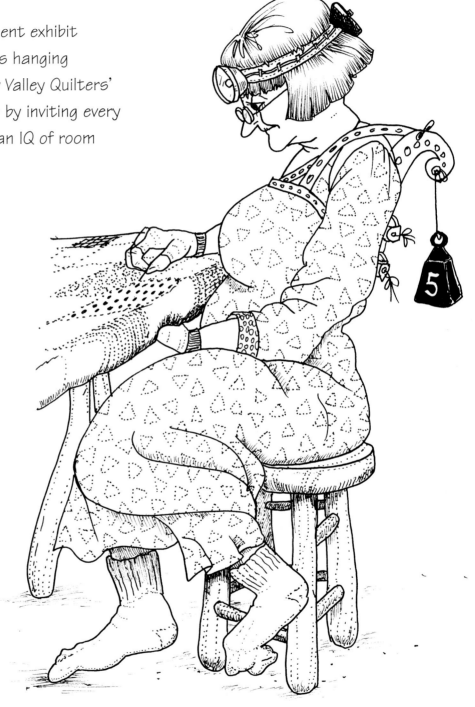

  Emma

There are 27 quilts hanging in the Grange; they started out with 30 but Joe Junior ran afoul of the law and his Mother, Emma, had to take her 3 quilts and sell them to some city folks who were staying in her Bed and Breakfast to bail his sorry behind out.

Emma's run her B&B, the Rooster's Resort, for 16 years but everyone in town knows she's only had people stay there about a dozen times - it's not on anyone's map. Plus, she only has one bathroom for herself, her son Joe, his wife and three kids and the "guests." Joe Senior was always going to put another bath in but while he was looking at plumbing fixtures and whatnots in Hastings Hardware he got "distracted," so Emma says, and left town that very night with Arlene Simpson and hasn't been seen

since. That's when Emma opened her B&B - it sort of took her mind off things. If more people knew about the Rooster's Resort they'd be booked solid because Emma makes the best homemade orange waffles with orange syrup you'll ever taste. Times have been hard for Emma but you'd never know it - if she ain't smilin' then it's only because her dentures have slipped. She is the happiest person in Happy Valley and never has an unkind word to say about anyone, especially that shiftless son of hers and her deadbeat husband.

Alice

About Alice…her bobbin's wound a little tight, you probably know the type.

When Eudora called to invite Alice to come to the quilt demonstration, Alice told her she was unable to attend because she had other plans that evening. Actually what she said was, "I'm stripping that night so you'll have to have your little meeting on another night!" You see, Alice belongs to a strip club over in Heber City, not the kind you're probably thinking - shame on you! - but the kind where you trade strips of fabric every month for quilting. Alice likes to pretend that her strip club is synonymous with high society and that her strip quilts are better than anybody's in Happy Valley because she has fabric from 47 states and Canada in her collection. She loves to introduce herself as a "stripper," just to get a reaction. And she got a reaction from Eudora that day, that's for sure! Apparently, Eudora was just about to tell Alice what she could do with her stripping when Alice announced she would boycott the meeting and then hung up. Why, you could hear all of Happy Valley talking the next morning about what those two said to each other without lifting your head off the pillow!

The day after the quilt meeting, Eudora ran into Alice at the Tack and Feed. Alice, to her credit, went right up to Eudora and in front of everyone said, "Dora, you'll have to forgive me for the other night, you know how much stripping means to me…I certainly didn't mean to be rude and I'd love to join your little group if you'll have me?" Eudora, who hates being called Dora, stared into Alice's eyes and sensing that the Tack and Feed had grown very silent she paused before

saying, "Why Alice, whatever do you mean? Of course you're welcome to join us. Next meeting will be at the Grange, I'll let you know when." With that they faked a hug and went their separate ways…but not before Eudora made a mental note to tell everyone that she smelled liquor on Alice's breath and it was only 10:00 in the morning!

There's always been friction between those two. In fact, Alice's middle name is friction! She is younger than Eudora, only 60 years old, and she has the body of a 30 year old, which is one reason Eudora gets a touch of the "green-eyed monster." Eudora can't walk within two feet of a piece of cheesecake without gaining a pound and Alice eats like there's no tomorrow and never gains an ounce. Most folks get along just fine with Alice

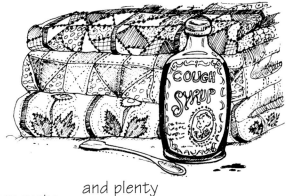

and plenty would trade places with her in a heartbeat - she's got style, money, a great husband with a full head of hair, and the largest collection of quilts this side of the Blue Mountains. Yes, she drinks, but only cough syrup for her constant bronchitis, which she blames on staying up late at night stripping. But Alice runs hot and cold, one minute she's singing your praises and the next, well, when you're on the wrong side of Alice it's kind of like being barefoot with cuts on your feet in the middle of the Salt flats - you're just afraid to move!

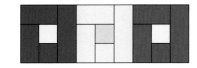

Beverly

Right past the Grange, across the street from the DQ is Beverly's Beauty Salon where you can get a shampoo and set for $4.95 if you're a regular - it'll set you back an even $10.00 if you're not.

Beverly lives upstairs, above the salon, which is why her place always smells like someone's having their hair permed. Beverly lives with nine cats, so between the perm smell and the cat hair it's always quite an experience to pay her a visit.

In the back room of the salon, she hosts Mah Jong games with about a dozen women every week. She learned to play Mah Jong after her husband passed. She's been a widow nearly 30 years now, almost as long as she's been quilting. She had Ned cremated, bought herself a black wardrobe and black luggage, then hired a black limousine to take her to the airport where she boarded a

Northwest flight to the Orient. She wanted to spread Ned's ashes as far away from Happy Valley as she could. (Ned was a drinker – everything BUT cough syrup – and while he never laid a hand on Bev he sure made her life miserable.)

In Singapore she purchased her first bolt of fabric and in Thailand she bought her tenth. By the time she reached Hong Kong she was calling herself a fabricolic! She stayed for a month and loved every minute of it. Ned was last "seen" floating in Canton Harbor and I'm sure after 30 years he now loves Hong Kong, too!

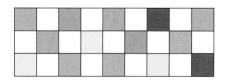

 # Mae

Beverly made friends with a local shop owner in Hong Kong, Mae, and she is the one who introduced her to Mah Jong.

After Beverly returned to Happy Valley, she stayed in contact with Mae and 10 years later Mae and her husband migrated to the States. If you look straight through Bev's back window to the green house across the street, you'll see Mae and Li Yang's red front door.

The Yangs were the talk of the town when they arrived back in '82. Fortunately they spoke English — or at least their version of English, which was a help to them when they opened the first and only Chinese restaurant in Happy Valley. Mae was a charter member of Happy Valley Quilters and was also instrumental in bringing Hong Kong Day to Happy Valley. It's always held the third Saturday in August, and Mae and Li cook for three days before this annual event. The doors open promptly at 5:00 for the "feast" and there is never an empty seat. The favorite part of the evening is trying to guess what everyone is eating and it just wouldn't be the same if old Mr. Williams didn't stand up and swear his dogs disappeared three days earlier! But Mae and Li take it all in stride and at the end of the evening Mae holds up a quilt and everyone ohhs and ahhs while Li tells the crowd to look under their seat for the gold star. The lucky person with the gold star goes home with one of Mae's beautiful quilts. Mae has been giving away a hand-made quilt for six years now — just her way of saying thanks for all the niceties that have been given to them.

  Inga

At the end of Main Street just before the Piney Creek Bridge is the dirt road cut-off that'll take you up to the Olson place.

Inga's family were the first settlers in Happy Valley. Inga went to elementary school, secondary, and high school at the Grange but left to go to college in Minnesota where she met and married Sven. They moved back to Happy Valley to take over the family business. Sven is the mayor, has been since 1968 and probably always will be. He's run unopposed in the last 14 elections. Inga, aside from being a mother of 6 with 36 grandchildren, is also the librarian at the new Olson Elementary School. She began quilting as a child and she manages to work the word "quilt" into every sentence she speaks. If you say you're having a bad day she'll tell you, "When life gives you scraps, make quilts." If you say it looks like it's going to rain, then she'll reply, "It does, but then there's nothing better to do during a rain storm than work on a quilt!" Can't argue with that! You might say she's obsessed, but she'll tell you that having a hobby is as necessary as breathing.

There's one more resident of Happy Valley that you should know about…Ginny.

She's not an actual resident but just try to tell her that. Her property lies directly three miles east of Happy Valley which puts her in Corinth County, and Happy Valley is located in Benton County, as any map will show. Ginny and her husband, Roger, moved into the old Chesterfield House on Elm right in the center of Happy Valley about 45 years ago. Roger opened the Happy Valley Funeral Home a few years later - in the lower level of the house. Ginny took care of greeting the bereaved and doing the make-up on the deceased - I guess you could call it a Mom and Pop business. Then the flood hit - the big one in '67.

Never seen anything like it before or after. Main Street was under water for three days and the Branch cousins, who passed four days before the flood due to a "hunting accident" (rumor has it they were hunting each other), were left floating in the Happy Valley Funeral Home. Mr. Branch, one of the uncles and the owner of the Happy Valley Bank, decided that the funeral home would not be able to secure funds to be

rebuilt - he was upset about his nephews floating around. So Ginny and Roger closed the funeral home and moved out of Happy Valley. They settled in Clayton and opened a new funeral parlor, which they called Happy Valley Funeral Parlor. Word had gotten out about the "floaters" during the flood so business wasn't too good at first - but things soon picked up. At some point everyone needs a funeral home!

Ginny

Roger is retired now and his son, Seth, runs the place. Who would have guessed that Seth would turn out to be such a marketing genius? He's the one who came up with the slogan, "Let's put the FUN back into FUNeral!"

Ginny has one remarkable talent, aside from quilting....she turns all one-syllable words into three-syllable words. It can take her a full twenty seconds to say, "There's a duck in the road over there!"

Eudora said that if a Lawrence Welk album were to play when Ginny spoke it would sound like she was singing along. But everyone loves Ginny - she's not afraid of anything, is always up for a little adventure, and she can quilt like nobody's business. She drives over to Happy Valley most every day, and always on Tuesday for Mah Jong and always on the last Friday of the month for the Happy Valley Quilters' meeting at the Grange.

Now that you've met everyone who's important in Happy Valley,
it's time you got to see some of the Happy Valley Quilters' quilts!

The gals got together and came up with some tips that should be read first. This was a matter of great discussion, as everyone has their own way of doing things, so if your way is different then you'd fit right in as a Happy Valley Quilter!

Also, all fabric requirements listed are generous amounts — you'll always have some left over to help you build your stash, or as Merle would say, your fabric library! Emma used to always buy just the exact amount and then when the group would do a round robin or a charity quilt she never had any scraps to donate — she learned the hard way — and her motto ever since has been, "You can't go wrong if you buy too much."

After deciding which quilt you are going to make, purchase your fabrics. In Happy Valley only 100% cotton fabric is used. If you want to use polyester fabric, well then you need to know it's going to pill and snag and it will never, ever be a quilt worth hangin' in the Grange! Prewashing your fabric is recommended since it will shrink, although there are plenty of quilters who just skip this step depending on the colors of the fabric they are using. Happy

Valley Quilters always prewash red fabrics — you just can't trust them not to bleed all over everything! All yardages of fabric given are based on 45" wide fabric and a little extra is allowed for the occasional mistake and/or scrap bag collection. Speaking of mistakes, if you make one and you need to unpick a seam, go right on ahead and do it. Unpick is the word of choice in Happy Valley...but if you want to say pick-out (like the Corinth County Quilters) instead of unpick then feel free — we're not linguists — just quilters and we all know what unpick means! All seam allowances are $1/4$" unless otherwise noted.

All appliqué shown is "needle-turn" appliqué. Trace the appliqué pieces onto the wrong side of the fabric. Cut out the pieces leaving a scant 1/4" seam allowance around each one. Using a water-soluble marking pen, trace the pattern onto the right side of the fabric where the appliqué pieces will go. Pin cut-out appliqué piece onto the right side of fabric into its position. Appliqué into place using matching thread and tiny, almost-invisible stitches. If you have a better method of appliqué, by all means use it.

When it's time to quilt your quilt, start by making the quilt "sandwich." Cut batting and backing fabric 8" larger than quilt top. Place backing (bottom of sandwich) right side down onto the floor or a large table and securely tape edges down, smoothing as you go. Place batting (the middle of the sandwich) on top of backing. Place quilt top (the top of the sandwich) down on top of the batting, right side up. Pin baste the 3 pieces together with quilter's safety pins (they're curved for easier use but regular ones will work just fine). Now you're ready to quilt by hand or machine quilt, either way is fine. Happy Valley Quilters used to only quilt by hand — and constantly argued about the value and beauty of machine quilted quilts. Then one day, Merle comes to the monthly meeting with a machine quilted baby quilt and you would have thought she'd walked in buck naked! There were audible gasps when she held this quilt up, but before anyone could say one word she proceeded to tell them that just because you machine quilt a quilt doesn't mean you're not a real quilter! Well, no one was going to argue with Merle and if machine quilting was good enough for her then it was good enough for them. Ever since then there's hardly been a monthly meeting where someone shows off a hand-quilted quilt — they're just too busy finishing all of those tops by machine to take the time to hand quilt!

Merle's
Hearts & Petals

Merle made her Hearts and Petals Quilt when Earl had his bypass surgery. She took the appliqué pieces with her each day to the hospital to keep her busy while Earl was plugged in like a GE appliance. That's the thing about appliqué, it is portable and Merle ported hers from the house to the hospital to the cafeteria for over two weeks and by the time Earl was home in his own easy chair Merle had all of the appliqué done.

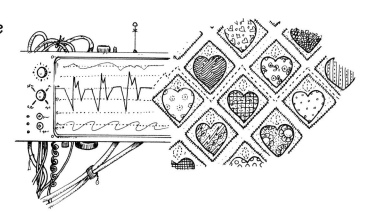

"I never met a quilter I didn't like."
Merle, 1989

 25

Quilt Size: 75$\frac{1}{2}$" x 75$\frac{1}{2}$" (192 x 192 cm)
Block Size: 10$\frac{1}{2}$" x 10$\frac{1}{2}$" (27 x 27 cm)

YARDAGE REQUIREMENTS

Yardage is based on 45" (114 cm) wide fabric.

6$\frac{3}{4}$ yds (6.2 m) of cream print
2 yds (1.8 m) of burgundy print #1
$\frac{3}{8}$ yd (34 cm) of burgundy print #2
$\frac{3}{8}$ yd (34 cm) of burgundy print #3
$\frac{1}{4}$ yd (23 cm) of green print
4$\frac{3}{4}$ yds (4.3 m) for backing
1 yd (91 cm) for binding

You will also need:

83" x 83" (211 x 211 cm)
  square of batting
Template plastic
Water- or air-soluble
  fabric pen

Read General Instructions first or just dive right in. Some of my best quilts came out of making mistakes!
—Merle

CUTTING OUT THE PIECES

*Refer to **Template Cutting**, page 85, to make templates for appliqué. Appliqué patterns are on page 28 and do not include seam allowance. Seam allowance should be added for traditional needle-turn appliqué. Follow **Rotary Cutting**, page 82, to cut fabric. Measurements listed include $\frac{1}{4}$" seam allowances.*

1. **From cream print:**
   - Cut 5 strips 11"w. From these strips, cut 13 **setting squares** 11" x 11".
   - Cut 4 strips 13"w. From these strips, cut 12 **large squares** 13" x 13".
   - Cut 2 *lengthwise* **top/bottom outer borders** 7" x 79".
   - Cut 2 *lengthwise* **side outer borders** 7" x 66".
   - Cut 2 squares 8$\frac{3}{8}$" x 8$\frac{3}{8}$". Cut squares *once* diagonally to make 4 **corner setting triangles**.
   - Cut 3 squares 16$\frac{1}{8}$" x 16$\frac{1}{8}$". Cut squares *twice* diagonally to make 12 **setting triangles**.

2. **From burgundy print #1:**
   - Cut 2 *lengthwise* **top/bottom inner borders** 1$\frac{1}{2}$" x 66".
   - Cut 2 *lengthwise* **side outer borders** 1$\frac{1}{2}$" x 64".
   - Cut 48 **hearts**.
   - Cut 48 **petals**.

3. **From burgundy print #2:**
   - Cut 96 **petals**.

4. **From burgundy print #3:**
   - Cut 96 **petals**.

5. **From green print:**
   - Cut 48 **stems**.

ASSEMBLING THE QUILT TOP

*Follow **Piecing**, page 85, **Pressing**, page 86, and **Needle-turn Appliqué**, page 86, to make quilt top.*

1. Using water- or air-soluble fabric pen, draw diagonal lines across 1 **large square** (**Fig. 1**). Using drawn lines as guide for appliqué placement, arrange **stems**, **hearts**, and **petals**; appliqué in place. Centering appliquéd design, trim square to 11" x 11" to make **Appliquéd Block**. Make 12 **Appliquéd Blocks**.

Fig. 1

Appliquéd Block (make 12)

2. Following **Quilt Top Center Assembly Diagram**, sew 12 **Appliquéd Blocks**, 13 **setting squares**, 12 **setting triangles**, and 4 **corner setting triangles** together to complete center section of quilt top.

3. Measure across *length* at center of **quilt top** and trim **side inner borders** to determined measurement. Sew **side inner borders** to quilt top.
4. Measure across *width* at center of quilt top, including added borders, and trim **top** and **bottom inner borders** to determined measurement. Sew **top** and **bottom inner borders** to quilt top.
5. In the same manner, add **outer borders** to complete quilt top.

COMPLETING THE QUILT
1. Follow **Quilting**, page 88, to mark, layer and quilt as desired. Our quilt is machine quilted. All of the cream areas (appliqué background, setting pieces, and outer border) are stipple quilted. The inner border and appliqués are not quilted.
2. Cut a 30" square of binding fabric. Follow **Binding**, page 92, to bind quilt using 2¹/₂"w bias binding with mitered corners.

Quilt Top Center Assembly Diagram

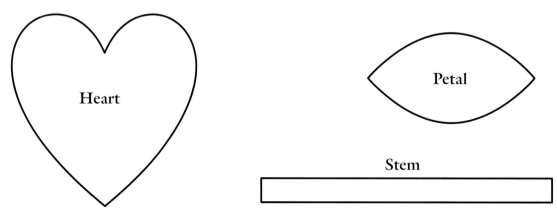

Heart

Petal

Stem

Merle's Green Apple Sour Cream Pie with Caramel Sauce

APPLE SOUR CREAM PIE

    4 cups thinly sliced, peeled Granny Smith apples
      (about 5 medium apples)
    3 tablespoons brown sugar
    2 tablespoons lemon juice
    1/4 cup butter
    4 ounces cream cheese, softened
    1 cup sour cream
    1 cup milk
    1 package (3.4 ounces) instant cheesecake
      pudding mix
    9-inch pie shell, baked

CARAMEL SAUCE

    1/2 cup sweetened condensed milk
    1/4 cup brown sugar
    1/4 cup dark corn syrup
    1 tablespoon butter
    1 teaspoon vanilla extract

In a large skillet over medium heat, sauté the apples, brown sugar and lemon juice in butter until apples are tender. Cool. In a medium mixing bowl, beat the cream cheese and sour cream until smooth. Gradually beat in milk and pudding mix; beat until thickened. Spread into pie shell. Arrange apples over filling. Refrigerate for one hour.

In a small saucepan over medium-high heat, combine milk, brown sugar and corn syrup. Whisking constantly, bring to a boil until thick, about 5 to 7 minutes. Remove from heat and add butter and vanilla; stir until smooth. Drizzle Caramel Sauce over top of apples and refrigerate for one hour longer before serving. Serves 8.

Eudora's French Revival

Eudora says her name means French Lady – it doesn't, but that's what she'll have you believe. She is a true Francophile - she loves everything French. She says she's French, too, French Cajun, that is, born in Paris, Georgia, and raised in the swamps of Louisiana - and how she got to Happy Valley is another story. She's lived here for close to 60 years now but when you enter her home you see where her heart is - French stuff everywhere. She has an Eiffel Tower puzzle that's been glued and framed over her davenport and an Eiffel Tower lamp from one of her great-grandsons. Her favorite chair has been upholstered in real French Toile that she ordered direct from a quilt shop in Paris and it was the inspiration for this French Revival Quilt. Eudora took the traditional French fabric and not wanting to cut away too much of the design she used big blocks and married them to a traditional American block, the Reel, for one of her finest quilts to date. And considering she's only been quilting for a few years, you can see why she's the guru of quilts in Happy Valley.

"When you've got cataracts all greens go together."
Eudora, 1996

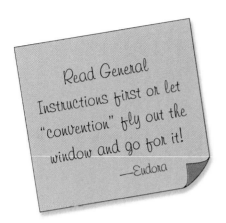

Read General Instructions first or let "convention" fly out the window and go for it!

—Eudora

Quilt Size: 62¹/₂" x 62¹/₂" (159 x 159 cm)
Block Size: 8¹/₂" x 8¹/₂" (22 x 22 cm)

YARDAGE REQUIREMENTS

Yardage is based on 45" (114 cm) wide fabric.

Red toile print [You will need enough toile print to center motifs in 12 squares 9" x 9" (23 x 23 cm).]

2¹/₄ yds (2.1 m) of cream print

⁵/₈ yds (57 cm) of red checked print

2³/₄ yd (2.5 m) of large red floral print

4 yds (3.7 m) for backing

⁷/₈ yd (80 cm) for binding

You will also need:

70" x 70" (178 x 178 cm) square of batting

Template plastic

Water- or air-soluble fabric pen

CUTTING OUT THE PIECES

*Refer to **Template Cutting**, page 85, to make templates for appliqué. Appliqué patterns are on page 34 and do not include seam allowance. Seam allowance should be added for traditional needle-turn appliqué. Follow **Rotary Cutting**, page 82, to cut fabric. Measurements listed include ¹/₄" seam allowances.*

1. **From toile print:**
    *   Cut 12 **setting blocks** 9" x 9", centering a motif on each square.

2. **From cream print:**
    *   Cut 4 *lengthwise* **inner border strips** 1¹/₂" x 47".
    *   Cut 13 **large squares** 12" x 12".

3. **From red checked print:**
    *   Cut 4 **border squares** 1¹/₂" x 1¹/₂".
    *   Cut 52 **swags**.

4. **From large red floral print:**
    *   Cut 2 *lengthwise* **top/bottom outer borders** 9" x 66".
    *   Cut 2 *lengthwise* **side outer borders** 9" x 49".
    *   Cut 13 **reels**.

ASSEMBLING THE QUILT TOP

*Follow **Piecing**, page 85, **Pressing**, page 86, and **Needle-turn Appliqué**, page 86, to make quilt top.*

1. Using water- or air-soluble fabric pen, draw diagonal lines across 1 **large square** (**Fig. 1**). Using drawn lines as guide for appliqué placement, arrange 4 **swags** and 1 **reel** onto square; appliqué in place. Centering appliquéd design, trim square to 9" x 9" to make **Appliquéd Block**. Make 13 **Appliquéd Blocks**.

Fig. 1

Appliquéd Block (make 13)

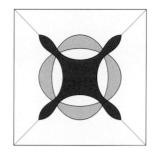

2. Sew 3 **Appliquéd Blocks** and 2 **setting blocks** together to make **Row A**. Make 3 **Row A's**.

3. Sew 2 **Appliquéd Blocks** and 3 **setting blocks** together to make **Row B**. Make 2 **Row B's**.

4. Alternating **Row A's** and **Row B's**, sew **Rows** together to complete center section of quilt top.

5. Measure across *width* at center of **quilt top** and trim 2 **inner border strips** to determined measurement. Sew 1 **border square** to each end of these **inner border strips** to make **top/bottom inner borders**.

6. Measure across *length* at center of quilt top and trim 2 **inner border strips** to determined measurement to make **side inner borders**.

7. Sew **side**, **top**, then **bottom inner borders** to quilt top.

8. Measure across *length* center of **quilt top** and trim **side outer borders** to determined measurement. Sew **side outer borders** to quilt top.

9. Measure across *width* at center of quilt top (including borders) and trim **top/bottom outer borders** to determined measurement. Sew **top/bottom outer borders** to quilt top.

COMPLETING THE QUILT

1. Follow **Quilting**, page 88, to mark, layer and quilt as desired. Our quilt is hand quilted. The inner border and appliquéd designs are outline quilted. The silhouette of the appliquéd design is quilted in each setting block. A scalloped pattern is quilted in the outer border.

2. Cut a 27" square of binding fabric. Follow **Binding**, page 92, to bind quilt using $2^{1}/_{2}$"w bias binding with mitered corners.

Quilt Top Diagram

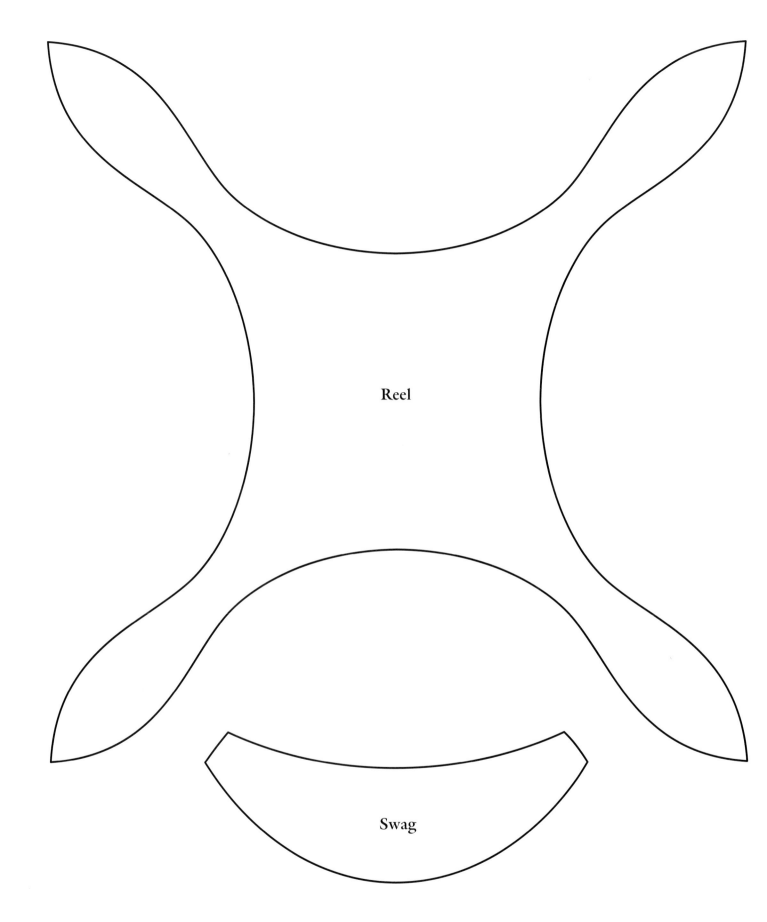

Reel

Swag

Eudora's **Cheese Grits Soufflé with Maple Sauce**

(OR AS SHE LIKES TO SAY – FRENCH GRITS)

GRITS

1 teaspoon salt
6 cups water
1¹/₂ cups quick-cooking grits
2 eggs
1¹/₂ cups shredded Cheddar cheese
dash of cayenne pepper
1 teaspoon black pepper
1 tablespoon butter
1 package (16 ounces) maple-flavored pork
  sausage, cooked and crumbled

MAPLE SYRUP SAUCE

¹/₂ cup ketchup
¹/₂ cup maple syrup

In a large sauce pan, add salt to water and bring to a boil. Gradually stir in grits; cover and reduce heat. Cook for 5 minutes, stirring occasionally; set aside. In a large bowl, beat eggs with a whisk. Add one cup of hot grits, whisking briskly so the eggs don't curdle/cook. Whisk egg mixture into pan of grits, mixing well. Add cheese, cayenne pepper, black pepper, butter and sausage. Stir until cheese and butter melt. Pour mixture into a buttered 2-quart soufflé dish. Bake in a 350-degree oven for 45 minutes or until grits are set and top is firm and golden brown. Let stand a full 5 minutes before serving.

Make Maple Syrup Sauce by combining ketchup and maple syrup. Drizzle over each individual serving or the soufflé. Serves 6 with big appetites and 8 with normal appetites!

Emma's Suzy Q

Emma has the most wonderful flower garden! She loves flowers, as you would see if you stayed at the Rooster Resort B&B. There isn't a wall that doesn't have floral wallpaper on it or a table that doesn't have a vase with flowers. Emma's boudoir is a collage of roses from her bed to her bath and her "swishy" caftans are all floral, too. She always looks like she's just about to bloom! That's why all of Emma's quilts have flowers in them and on them. When her shiftless, no-good, lazy-glutton-of-a-son had his third child, Emma decided to make this quilt for her new granddaughter, who is called Suzy Q. Q is her middle name, stands for Q, that's it, nothin' more. Suzy Q has her grandma's eyes and with any luck at all she'll have her grandma's talents, too!

"You can't go wrong if you buy too much!"

Emma, 1998

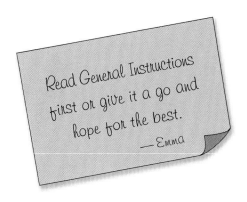

Read General Instructions first or give it a go and hope for the best.

—Emma

Quilt Size: 49³/₄" x 58" (126 x 147 cm)
Block Size: 5¹/₂" x 5¹/₂" (14 x 14 cm)

YARDAGE REQUIREMENTS

Yardage is based on 45" (114 cm) wide fabric.

1⁵/₈ yds (1.5 m) of cream print
³/₈ yd (34 cm) of tan floral print
1¹/₄ yds (1.1 m) of rust polka-dot print
  (includes binding)
¹/₈ yd (11 cm) of tan stripe print
1 yd (91 cm) *total* of assorted green prints
1 yd (91 cm) *total* of assorted tan prints
³/₄ yd (69 cm) *total* of assorted rust prints
¹/₄ yd (23 cm) rust floral print
3³/₄ yds (3.4 m) for backing

You will also need:

58" x 66" (147 x 168 cm) piece of batting
Template plastic

CUTTING OUT THE PIECES

*Refer to **Template Cutting**, page 85, to make templates for appliqué. Appliqué patterns are on page 42 and do not include seam allowance. Seam allowance should be added for traditional needle-turn appliqué. Follow **Rotary Cutting**, page 82, to cut fabric. Measurements listed include ¹/₄" seam allowances. Borders are cut exact length needed.*

1. **From cream print:**
   - Cut 3 strips 8"w. From these strips, cut 14 **large squares** 8" x 8"
   - Cut 1 strip 9¹/₈"w. From this strip, cut 3 squares 9¹/₈" x 9¹/₈". Cut squares *twice* diagonally, to make 12 **setting triangles**. (You will use 10 and have 2 left over.)
   - Cut 4 strips 3¹/₄"w. From these strips, cut 42 **small squares** 3¹/₄" x 3¹/₄".
   - Cut 2 squares 4⁷/₈" x 4⁷/₈". Cut squares *once* diagonally to make 4 **corner setting triangles**.

2. **From tan floral print:**
   - Cut 2 strips 6" wide. From these strips, cut 12 **setting squares** 6" x 6".

3. **From rust polka-dot print:**
   - Cut 2 **side 1st borders** ⁷/₈" x 31⁵/₈".
   - Cut 13 strips 1"w. From these strips:
     - Cut 2 **top/bottom 1st borders** 1" x 24⁵/₈".
     - Cut 2 **side 3rd borders** 1" x 33⁵/₈".
     - Cut 2 **top/bottom 3rd borders** 1" x 26³/₈".
     - Cut 2 **top/bottom 5th borders** 1" x 38¹/₄".
     - Sew 3 strips together lengthwise to make 1 strip. From this strip, cut 2 **side 5th borders** 1" x 45¹/₂".
     - Cut 16 **sashings** 1" x 6"
   - Cut 1 **square for binding** 26" x 26".

4. **From tan stripe:**
   - Cut 2 **side 2nd borders** ⁷/₈" x 32⁵/₈".
   - Cut 2 **top/bottom 2nd borders** 1" x 25³/₈".

5. **From assorted green prints:**
   - Cut 14 **small squares** 3¹/₄" x 3¹/₄".
   - Cut 42 **leaves**.
     *Set aside remaining assorted prints for **6th borders**.*

6. **From assorted tan prints:**
   - Cut 14 **small squares** $3^1/4$" x $3^1/4$".
   - Cut 6 **small flower centers**.
   - Cut 8 **large flower centers**.
     Set aside remaining assorted prints for ***6th borders***.
7. **From assorted rust prints:**
   - Cut 14 **small squares** $3^1/4$" x $3^1/4$".
     Set aside remaining assorted prints for ***6th borders***.
8. **From rust floral print:**
   - Cut 6 **small flowers**.
   - Cut 8 **large flowers**.

ASSEMBLING THE QUILT TOP
*Follow **Piecing**, page 85, **Pressing**, page 86, and **Needle-turn Appliqué**, page 86, to make quilt top.*

1. Arrange 3 **leaves**, 1 **small flower**, and 1 **small flower center** on 1 **large square**; appliqué. Centering appliquéd design, trim square to 6" x 6" to make **Appliquéd Block**. Make 6 **Appliquéd Blocks**.

Appliquéd Block (make 6)

2. Arrange 3 **leaves**, 1 **large flower**, and 1 **large flower center** on 1 **large square**; appliqué. Centering appliquéd design, trim square to 6" x 6" to make **Appliquéd Corner Square**. Make 8 **Appliquéd Corner Squares**.

Appliquéd Corner Square (make 8)

3. Following **Quilt Top Center Assembly Diagram**, sew 6 **Appliquéd Blocks**, 12 **setting squares**, 10 **setting triangles**, and 4 **corner setting triangles** together to complete center section of quilt top.

Quilt Top Center Assembly Diagram

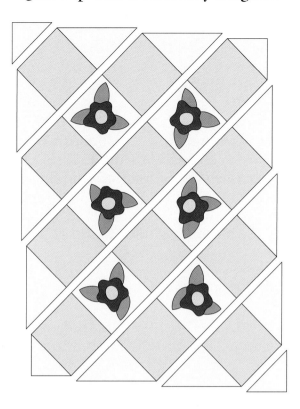

4. Sew **side**, **top**, then **bottom 1st borders** to quilt top center. Repeat to add **2nd** and **3rd borders**.

5. Sew 1 cream **small square** and 1 assorted print **small square** together to make **Unit 1**. Make 42 **Unit 1's**.

Unit 1 (make 42)

6. Sew 12 **Unit 1's** together to make **Unit 2**.

Unit 2 (make 2)

7. Sew 9 **Unit 1's** together to make **Unit 3**. Make 2 **Unit 3's**.

Unit 3 (make 2)

8. Sew 1 **sashing** to each end of **Unit 2** to make **side 4th border**. Make 2 **side 4th borders**.

Side 4th Border (make 2)

9. Sew 1 **sashing**, then 1 **Appliquéd Corner Square** to each end of **Unit 3** to make **fourth top border**. Repeat to make **4th bottom border**.

Top/Bottom 4th Border (make 2)

10. Sew **side**, **top**, then **bottom 4th borders** to quilt top. Repeat to add **5th borders**.

11. Cut 6" rectangles of various widths ($^3/_4$" to $1^3/_4$") from remaining green, rust, and tan prints. Sew enough rectangles together to make 2 **Unit 4's** 6" x $45^1/_2$". Sew enough rectangles together to make 2 **Unit 5's** 6" x $37^1/_4$".

Unit 4 (make 2)

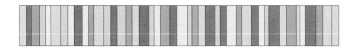

Unit 5 (make 2)

12. Sew 1 **sashing** to each end of **Unit 4** to make **side 6th border**. Make 2 **side 6th borders**.

Side 6th Border (make 2)

13. Sew 1 **sashing**, then 1 **Appliquéd Corner Square** to each end of **Unit 5** to make **6th top border**. Repeat to make **6th bottom border.**

Top/Bottom 6th Border (make 2)

14. Add **side, top**, then **bottom 6th borders** to quilt top.

COMPLETING THE QUILT

1. Follow **Quilting**, page 88, to mark, layer and quilt as desired. Our quilt is machine quilted. The entire quilt, except for the appliqués, is stipple quilted. The appliqués are not quilted.

2. Using **square for binding**, follow **Binding**, page 92, to bind quilt using $2^1/_2$"w bias binding with mitered corners.

Quilt Top Diagram

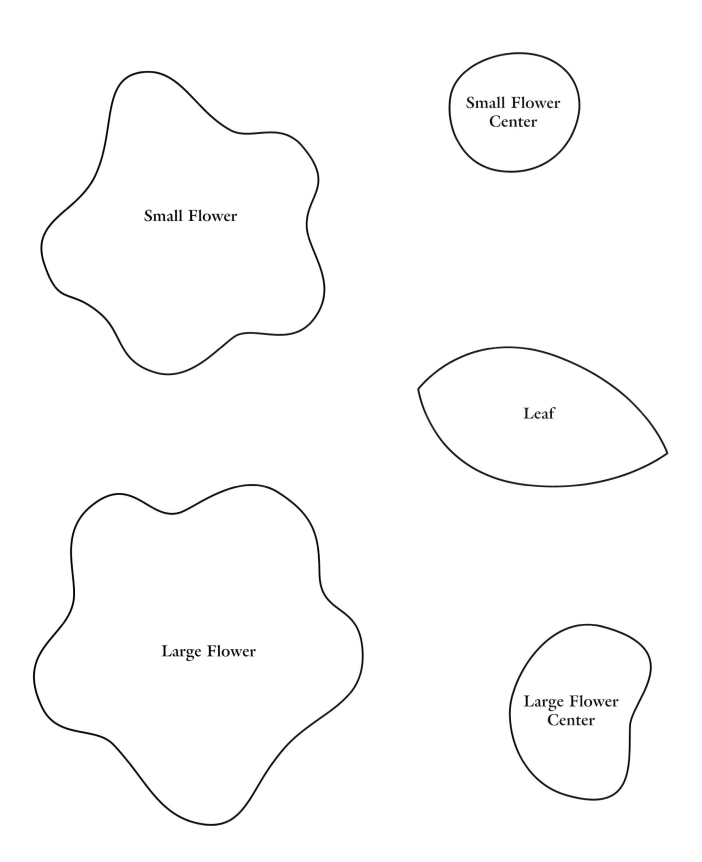

Small Flower Center

Small Flower

Leaf

Large Flower

Large Flower Center

Emma's Orange Waffles with Orange Syrup

Emma's secret for getting everyone hot waffles at the same time? She uses 3 waffle makers — bought them all at garage sales, too!

ORANGE WAFFLES

    2 cups flour
    2 tablespoons light brown sugar
    1 tablespoon baking powder
    1/2 teaspoon salt
    3 large eggs, separated
    1 cup half and half
    1/4 cup frozen orange juice concentrate
    1/2 cup melted butter
    1 can (11 ounces) mandarin orange segments,
      drained

ORANGE SYRUP

    2 cans (11 ounces each) mandarin orange
      segments (drain one can; reserve juice of the
      second can)
    1 tablespoon cornstarch
    1/4 cup butter

Preheat waffle iron. Combine flour, brown sugar, baking powder and salt; set aside. In a small bowl, whisk together egg yolks (reserve whites), half and half, orange juice concentrate and melted butter. Add mandarin oranges, squeezing by hand, so that the oranges are "squished" and all of the juices are released. Mix well; set aside. In a separate bowl, beat egg whites until stiff peaks form. Stir flour mixture into the orange mixture and mix well. Fold in egg whites with wooden spoon until blended. Pour 1/2 to 1 cup of batter into waffle iron (depending on the size of your waffle iron). Cook until golden brown in color, about 3 minutes.

Meanwhile, in a small saucepan, make the orange syrup. Drain one can of oranges only and add both cans of mandarin oranges to the saucepan. Squeeze oranges by hand to "squish" the oranges. Add cornstarch and butter and cook over medium-high heat until mixture thickens. Serve hot over waffles. Serves 4 to 6.

Alice's Square Deal

What more can be said about stripping? It's truly an art form and Alice has taken it to its highest level. She would rather strip than almost anything else and her strip club is one of the most active in a four-state region. Each month they trade a dozen or more strips of fabric just in the first round of stripping and they usually have ten rounds per meeting! Alice wears her rotary cutter on a chain around her neck, along with her glasses and a pair of scissors. She is so used to wearing this stuff dangling every which way that she just thinks of it as her jewelry and puts it on in the morning along with her watch and her earrings. The Happy Valley Quilters are happy she wears all of this stuff, too, because they can hear her coming like a cat wearing a bell, and it gives them plenty of time to look busy or make a mad dash to the rest room if they think she might be cross with them over something.

Alice made this quilt for her family room where she can be found of an evening watching Wheel of Fortune and then Jeopardy, her favorite TV shows.

"If you can strip you'll never be bored!"
Alice, 1997

Quilt Size: 61" x 61" (155 x 155 cm)
Block Size: 6³/₈" x 6³/₈" (16 x 16 cm)

YARDAGE REQUIREMENTS

Yardage is based on 45" (114 cm) wide fabric.
2¹/₂ yds (2.3 m) *total* of assorted prints
1⁷/₈ yds (1.7 m) of tan solid
1¹/₂ yds (1.4 m) of black solid
3⁷/₈ yds (3.5 m) for backing
⁷/₈ yd (80 cm) for binding
You will also need:
68" x 68" (173 x 173 cm) square of batting

Read General Instructions first or jump right in and start stripping!
—Alice

CUTTING OUT THE PIECES

*Follow **Rotary Cutting**, page 82, to cut fabric.*
Measurements listed include ¹/₄" seam allowances.
Borders are cut exact length needed.

1. **From assorted prints, cut the following for each set from one fabric. You will need a total of 49 sets.**
   - Cut 1 **square** 2⁵/₈" x 2⁵/₈".
   - Cut 2 **small rectangles** 2⁵/₈" x 4³/₄".
   - Cut 1 **large rectangle** 2⁵/₈" x 6⁷/₈".

   Also, from assorted prints:
   - Cut 77 **border** and **center squares** 2⁵/₈" x 2⁵/₈".

2. **From tan solid:**
   - Cut 2 *lengthwise* **top/bottom 4th borders** 2⁵/₈" x 60⁵/₈".
   - Cut 2 *lengthwise* **side 4th borders** 2⁵/₈" x 56³/₈".
   - Cut 2 *lengthwise* **top/bottom 2nd borders** 2⁵/₈" x 52¹/₈".
   - Cut 2 *lengthwise* **side 2nd borders** 2⁵/₈" x 47⁷/₈".

   From remaining width of fabric:
   - Cut 10 strips 2⁵/₈"w. From these strips:
     - Cut 24 **small border rectangles** 2⁵/₈" x 4³/₄".
     - Cut 4 **medium border rectangles** 2⁵/₈" x 6¹/₈".
     - Cut 4 **large border rectangles** 2⁵/₈" x 8¹/₄".

3. **From black solid:**
   - Cut 2 *lengthwise* **top/bottom 1st borders** 1⁷/₈" x 47⁷/₈".
   - Cut 2 *lengthwise* **side 1st borders** 1⁷/₈" x 45¹/₈".

Tip from Alice

Always cut the selvage edges off your fabric and don't use it in your quilts. Selvage has a very tight weave and it will react (shrink) differently than the rest of the fabric when washed.

ASSEMBLING THE QUILT TOP

*Follow **Piecing**, page 85, and **Pressing**, page 86, to make quilt top.*

1. Select 1 set from assorted fabrics (1 **square**, 2 **small rectangles**, and 1 **large rectangle**) and 1 contrasting **center square** for each **Block**. Following **Block Assembly Diagram**, make 1 **Block**. Repeat to make 49 **Blocks**.

Block Assembly Diagram

Block (make 49)

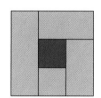

2. Sew 7 **Blocks** together to make **Row**. Make 7 **Rows**.

3. Sew **Rows** together to complete center section of quilt top.

4. Sew **side**, **top**, then **bottom 1st borders** to center section of quilt top. Repeat to add **2nd borders**.

5. Alternating 7 **border squares** and 6 **small border rectangles**, make **Unit 1**. Make 4 **Unit 1's**.

6. Sew 1 **large border rectangle** to each end of 1 **Unit 1** to make **top 3rd border**. Repeat to make **bottom 3rd border**.

7. Sew 1 **medium rectangle** to each end of remaining **Unit 1's** to make **side 3rd borders**.

8. Sew **side**, **top**, then **bottom 3rd borders** to quilt top. Repeat to add **4th borders**.

COMPLETING THE QUILT

1. Follow **Quilting**, page 88, to mark, layer and quilt as desired. Our quilt is machine quilted. The center section and outer 3 borders are meander quilted. The 1st border is not quilted.

2. Cut a 27" square of binding fabric. Follow **Binding**, page 92, to bind quilt using 2¹/₂"w bias binding with mitered corners.

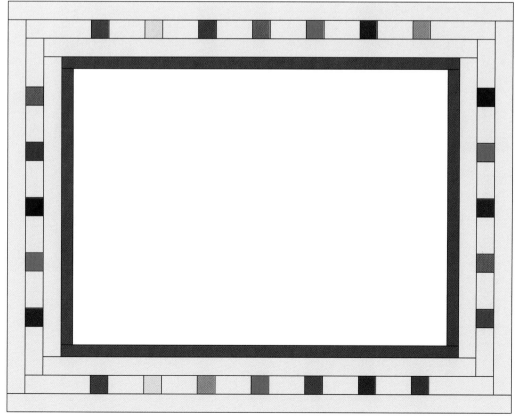

Trace, scan, or photocopy this quilt label to finish your quilt.

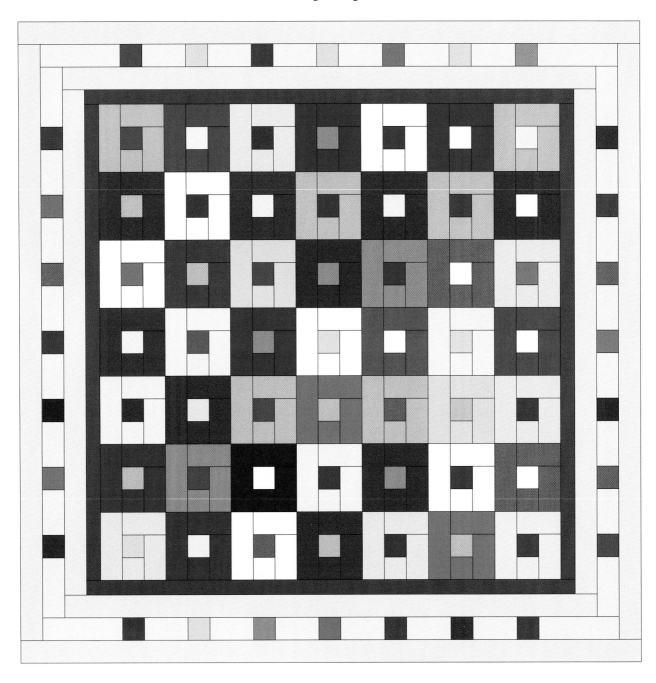

Alice's Sewing Tips

Since Alice doesn't cook, she didn't have a recipe to include. She only uses the microwave; her stovetop has been permanently covered up with a cutting mat for seven years now and that's where she does most of her stripping. So she submitted her best sewing tips instead and well, why not? She's got a few good ones that you might want to take note of!

IRONING TIPS

- Don't ever iron your quilts once they're quilted; the batting will become flatter than road kill and may even fuse the top and bottom of your quilt unevenly.

- I know you all know this but it's worth repeating: to clean your iron place a brown paper bag on the ironing board and sprinkle the bag with salt. Then iron the salt to make your iron nice and clean. Carefully fold the bag in half and pour the salt into a cup to save for another cleaning or to use in your garden on those pesky slugs!

- Another word about ironing...don't be pressing everything to death with your iron when a finger press will do. You can stretch your fabric by ironing it wrong, especially if you're working with triangles. Since triangles are bias (a true four-letter word if there ever was one), they are very stretchy - why, I've had some triangle patches stretch as much as half an inch just by ironing the wrong way! Never go back and forth with an iron when pressing triangles - go up and down. And press seams to the darkest fabric side - not open - they'll be stronger this way.

Recipe book holder = Quilt book holder

Dig out the plastic recipe book holder in the back of your kitchen cupboard and use it in your sewing room to hold your quilt book open as you sew.

Hanging Method

Alice uses a clever "hanger" she devised to hang up her strips of fabric. She mounted a 2" x 36" piece of wood to her workroom wall and pounded nails in it every 4 inches. She uses the Acco brand paper clips to hold her fabric strips and then hangs them on the nails. This way she can keep her strips wrinkle free until she uses them and she can see her wonderful fabrics at the same time! If you don't want to fuss with making Alice's device, skirt hangers work just as well, too.

Beverly's Baby Blooms Around the Coop

Beverly's granddaughter came as a complete surprise to all parties involved and is nicknamed Coop because of her auspicious beginning. One night just after sunset the sheriff was responding to a call about vandals. He drove up to the chicken coop behind the beauty parlor and shined his light inside – right on Bev's son and daughter-in-law...they were smack-dab in the middle of you-know-what and the sheriff had himself a good laugh before he turned off the light and drove over to Beverly's to tell her the chickens were safe but there might be an egg or two missing! Nine months later little Coop was born and Bev made this baby quilt for her.

*"Made for little Coop by Grandma Bev.
Sometimes a surprise is a wonderful blessing in disguise"*

Quilt Size: 42" x 43" (107 x 109 cm)

YARDAGE REQUIREMENTS

Yardage is based on 45" (114 cm) wide fabric.

$1^3/_4$ yds (1.6 m) of white print

$^1/_8$ yd (11 cm) *each* of 11 assorted small prints (including at least 3 green prints)

$^1/_4$ yd (23 cm) of pink print

$^3/_8$ yd (34 cm) of green print

$2^7/_8$ yds (2.6 m) for backing

$^3/_4$ yd (69 cm) for binding

You will also need:

50" x 51" (127 x 130 cm) piece of batting

Template plastic

Read General Instructions first or trust your instincts and keep going.

—Bev

CUTTING OUT THE PIECES

*Refer to **Template Cutting**, page 85, to make templates for appliqué. Appliqué patterns are on page 54 and do not include seam allowance. Seam allowance should be added for traditional needle-turn appliqué. Follow **Rotary Cutting**, page 82, to cut fabric. Measurements listed include $^1/_4$" seam allowances. Borders are cut exact length needed.*

1. **From white print:**
   - Cut 9 strips $1^1/_2$"w. From these strips:
     - Cut 11 **strips** $1^1/_2$"w x 21".
     - Cut 48 **rectangles** $1^1/_2$" x $2^1/_2$".
     - Cut 2 **squares** $1^1/_2$" x $1^1/_2$".
   - Cut 2 **side 2nd borders** 1" x $19^1/_2$".
   - Cut 2 **top/bottom 2nd borders** 1" x $17^1/_2$".
   - Cut 2 **side 4th borders** $4^1/_2$" x $30^1/_2$".
   - Cut 2 **top/bottom 4th borders** $4^1/_2$" x $21^1/_2$".
   - Cut 2 **side 6th borders** $2^1/_2$" x $36^1/_2$".
   - Cut 2 **top/bottom 6th borders** $2^1/_2$" x $31^1/_2$"
   - Cut 2 **side 8th borders** $2^1/_2$" x $42^1/_2$" (piecing if necessary).
   - Cut 2 **top/bottom 8th borders** $2^1/_2$" x $37^1/_2$".

2. **From assorted small prints:**
   - Cut 11 strips $1^1/_2$"w (1 from each print). From these strips:
     - Cut 11 **strips** $1^1/_2$" x 21" (1 from each print).
     - Cut 48 **squares** $1^1/_2$" x $1^1/_2$".
   - Cut 12 **flowers**.
   - Cut 12 (green) **leaves**.
   - Cut 12 (green) **stems**.

3. **From pink print:**
   - Cut 2 **side 5th borders** $1^1/_2$" x $32^1/_2$".
   - Cut 2 **top/bottom 5th borders** $1^1/_2$" x $29^1/_2$".

4. **From green print:**
   - Cut 2 **side 1st borders** 1" x $18^1/_2$".
   - Cut 2 **top/bottom 1st borders** 1" x $16^1/_2$".
   - Cut 2 **side 3rd borders** 2" x $22^1/_2$".
   - Cut 2 **top/bottom 3rd borders** 2" x $18^1/_2$".

ASSEMBLING THE QUILT TOP

*Follow **Piecing**, page 85, **Pressing**, page 86, and **Needle-turn Appliqué**, page 86, to make quilt top.*

1. Sew 1 assorted print **strip** and 1 white print **strip** together to make **strip set**. Make 11 **strip sets** using 1 print from assorted prints and 1 white print.

Strip Set

2. Cut across each **strip set** at $1^1/2$" intervals to make **Unit 1**. Make a total of 136 **Unit 1's**.

Unit 1 (make 136)

3. Sew 8 **Unit 1's** together in random order to make **Row**. Make 17 **Rows**.

Row (make 17)

4. Rotating every other **Row**, sew **Rows** together to complete center section of quilt top.

Center Section of Quilt Top

5. Sew **top**, **bottom**, then **side 1st borders** to center section of quilt top. Repeat to add **2nd** and **3rd borders** to quilt top.

6. Matching bottoms of **stems** to 1 long edge of **border**, appliqué 3 **stems**, 3 **leaves**, and 3 **flowers** on each **4th border**.

4th Border Appliqué Diagrams

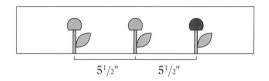

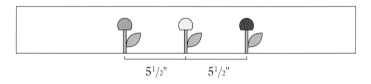

7. Sew **top**, **bottom**, then **side 4th borders** to center section of quilt top. Repeat to add **5th** and **6th borders** to quilt top.

8. Alternating **rectangles** and **squares**, sew 12 white print **rectangles** and 11 assorted print **squares** together to make **top 7th border**. Repeat to make **bottom 7th border**.

7th Top/Bottom Border

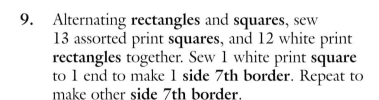

9. Alternating **rectangles** and **squares**, sew 13 assorted print **squares**, and 12 white print **rectangles** together. Sew 1 white print **square** to 1 end to make 1 **side 7th border**. Repeat to make other **side 7th border**.

7th Side Border

10. Sew **top**, **bottom**, then **side 7th borders** to quilt top. Repeat to add **8th borders** to quilt top.

COMPLETING THE QUILT

1. Follow **Quilting**, page 88, to mark, layer and quilt as desired. Our quilt is machine quilted. The squares in the center section and the first 5 borders are quilted in the ditch. The 4th and 7th borders are stipple quilted in the white areas.

2. Cut a 23" square of binding fabric. Follow **Binding**, page 92, to bind quilt using 2¹/₂"w bias binding with mitered corners.

Quilt Top Diagram

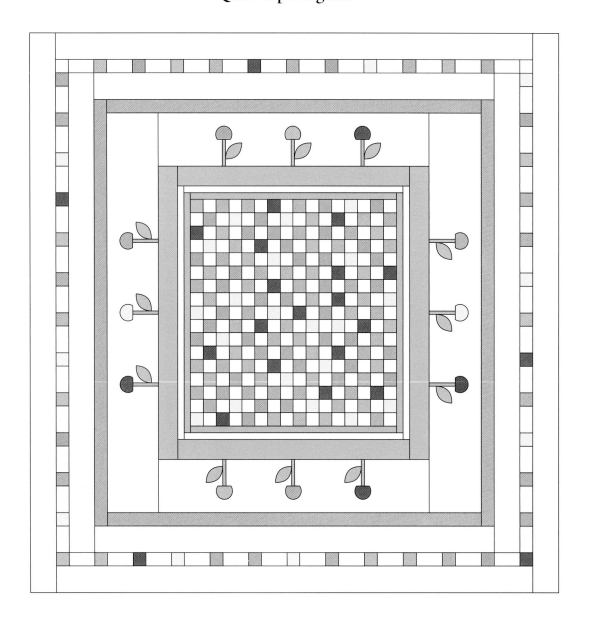

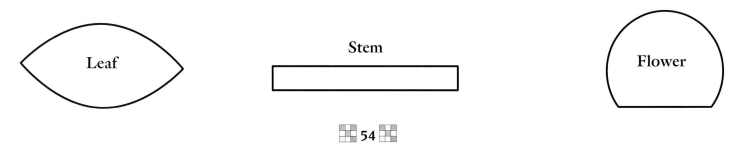

Leaf

Stem

Flower

Beverly's Hot Orange Cream Punch for Mah Jong Tuesdays

Plan on making more than you really need, because this is so good your guests will all want more!

4 cups orange juice
2 cinnamon sticks
1 tablespoon vanilla extract
1 pint vanilla ice cream
miniature marshmallows for serving

In a large saucepan, combine orange juice and cinnamon sticks over medium-high heat. Bring to a boil, then reduce to low heat. Simmer 10 minutes. Remove cinnamon sticks and stir in vanilla and ice cream. Cook over low heat, stirring constantly, until heated through. Do not allow to boil. Serve in mugs with mini marshmallows.
Serves 6 to 8.

Beverly's Springtime in the Valley

After Bev made her granddaughter a quilt, she liked how it turned out so much that she made another one almost like it - in fact, all of Bev's quilts look the same. She kind of gets into ruts, like the time she made nothing but Log Cabin quilts for six years. Everyone in her family, including second cousins, have a Log Cabin quilt from her. Then she stopped making them, just like that, and started making quilts like the one she made for little Coop and this one here - she's into little squares and you can see why, they're just as cute as can be! This quilt hangs in her guest bedroom right next to the velvet painting of Elvis.

"It's our patriotic duty to purchase fabric – we need to
keep the economy going, and help to protect the jobs of textile
mill workers and quilt shop employees everywhere!"
Beverly, 2001

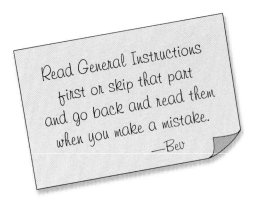

Read General Instructions first or skip that part and go back and read them when you make a mistake.

—Bev

Quilt Size: 51$\frac{1}{4}$" x 51$\frac{1}{4}$" (130 x 130 cm)

YARDAGE REQUIREMENTS

Yardage is based on 45" (114 cm) wide fabric.
   1 yd (91 cm) of white solid
   $\frac{1}{2}$ yd (46 cm) of green gingham print
   1$\frac{5}{8}$ yds (1.5 m) of green and yellow
      floral print
   1$\frac{1}{2}$ yds (1.4 m) of yellow print
   $\frac{1}{4}$ yd (23 cm) of pink floral print
   $\frac{1}{2}$ yd (46 cm) *total* of assorted pastel
      stripe prints
   3$\frac{3}{8}$ yds (3.1 m) for backing
   $\frac{3}{4}$ yd (69 cm) for binding
You will also need:
   59" x 59" (150 x 150 cm) square of batting
   Template plastic

CUTTING OUT THE PIECES

*Refer to **Template Cutting**, page 85, to make templates for appliqué. Appliqué patterns are on page 62 and do not include seam allowance. Seam allowance should be added for traditional needle-turn appliqué. Follow **Rotary Cutting**, page 82, to cut fabric. Measurements listed include $\frac{1}{4}$" seam allowances. Borders are cut exact length needed.*

1. **From white solid:**
    *   Cut 1 strip 7$\frac{1}{2}$"w. From this strip, cut **4 large squares** 7$\frac{1}{2}$" x 7$\frac{1}{2}$".
    *   Cut 2 **side 2nd borders** 8" x 29$\frac{3}{4}$".
    *   Cut 2 **top/bottom 2nd borders** 8" x 18$\frac{3}{4}$".

2. **From green gingham print:**
    *   Cut 4 **1st borders** 2$\frac{1}{8}$" x 18$\frac{3}{4}$".
    *   Cut 4 **vines**.
    *   Cut 4 **large leaves**.
    Set aside remaining green gingham.

3. **From green and yellow floral print:**
    *   Cut 2 *lengthwise* **side 7th borders** 2$\frac{1}{8}$" x 50$\frac{3}{4}$".
    *   Cut 2 *lengthwise* **top/bottom 7th borders** 2$\frac{1}{8}$" x 47$\frac{1}{2}$".
    *   Cut 2 *lengthwise* **side 3rd borders** 2$\frac{1}{8}$" x 31".
    *   Cut 2 *lengthwise* **top/bottom 3rd borders** 2$\frac{1}{8}$" x 27$\frac{3}{4}$".
    *   Cut 4 **flower centers**.
    Set aside remaining green and yellow floral print.

4. **From yellow print:**
    *   Cut 2 *lengthwise* **side 6th borders** 2$\frac{1}{8}$" x 47$\frac{1}{2}$".
    *   Cut 2 *lengthwise* **top/bottom 6th borders** 2$\frac{1}{8}$" x 44$\frac{1}{4}$".
    *   Cut 2 *lengthwise* **side 4th borders** 2$\frac{1}{8}$" x 34$\frac{1}{4}$".
    *   Cut 2 *lengthwise* **top/bottom 4th borders** 2$\frac{1}{8}$" x 31".
    Set aside remaining yellow print.

5. From pink floral print:
   - Cut 16 **large petals**.
   - Cut 16 **small petals**.
   Set aside remaining pink floral.
6. From assorted pastel stripes and reserved fabrics listed above:
   - Cut 108 **rectangles** $1^3/4$" x $5^1/2$".
   - Cut 64 **small squares** $2^1/8$" x $2^1/8$".
   - Cut 24 **small leaves**.

ASSEMBLING THE QUILT TOP
*Follow **Piecing**, page 85, **Pressing**, page 86, and **Needle-turn Appliqué**, page 86, to make quilt top.*

1. In random color order, sew 8 **small squares** together to make **Row**. Make 8 **Rows**.

Row (make 8)

2. Sew 8 **Rows** together to complete center section of quilt top.

Center Section of Quilt Top

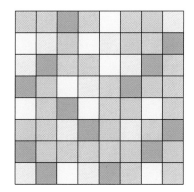

3. The **1st borders** are mitered. Center and stitch **1st borders** to center section of quilt top, beginning and ending seams *exactly* $1/4$" from each corner of quilt top center section. Backstitch at beginning and ending of stitching to reinforce. Fold one corner of quilt top diagonally with right sides together

and matching edges. Use ruler to mark stitching line as shown in **Mitered Corner Diagram**. Sew on drawn line, backstitching at beginning and ending of stitching. Trim seam allowance to $1/4$" and press to one side. Repeat for other corners.

Mitered Corner Diagram

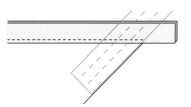

4. Center 1 **vine** on **top 2nd border**; appliqué in place. Appliqué 6 **small leaves** along vine. Repeat for **bottom 2nd border**. Trim **borders** to 6" x $16^3/4$".

Top/Bottom 2nd Border Appliqué Diagram

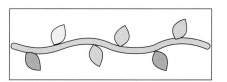

5. Center 1 **vine** on 1 **side 2nd border**; appliqué in place. Appliqué 6 **small leaves** along **vine**. Arrange flower (3 **large petals**, 2 **small petals**, and 1 **flower center**) on each end of vine 2" from raw edges; appliqué in place. Repeat for other **side 2nd border**. Trim **borders** to 6" x $27^3/4$".

Side 2nd Border Appliqué Diagram

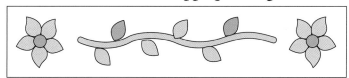

6. In center of **large square**, appliqué 1 **large petal**, 2 **small petals**, and 1 **large leaf**. Repeat for remaining 3 **large squares**. Trim **large squares** to $5^1/2$" x $5^1/2$".

Large Square Appliqué Diagram

7. In random color order, sew 27 **rectangles** together to make **5th borders**. Sew appliquéd **large square** to each end of 2 **side 5th borders**.

Top/Bottom 5th Border

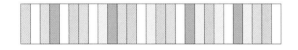

Side 5th Border

8. Sew **top**, **bottom**, then **side 2nd borders** to center section of quilt top. Repeat to add **3rd** through **7th borders** to complete quilt top.

COMPLETING THE QUILT

1. Follow **Quilting**, page 88, to mark, layer and quilt as desired. Our quilt is hand quilted. The white areas are filled with echo quilting around the appliqués. The remainder of the quilt is outline quilted.

2. Cut a 25" square of binding fabric. Follow **Binding**, page 92, to bind quilt using $2^1/2$"w bias binding with mitered corners.

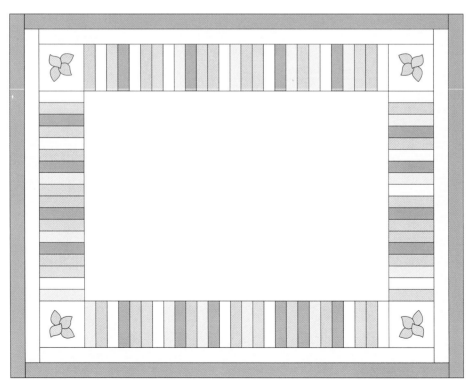

Trace, scan, or photocopy this quilt label to finish your quilt.

Leisure Arts, Inc., grants permission to photocopy this page for personal use only.

Quilt Top Diagram

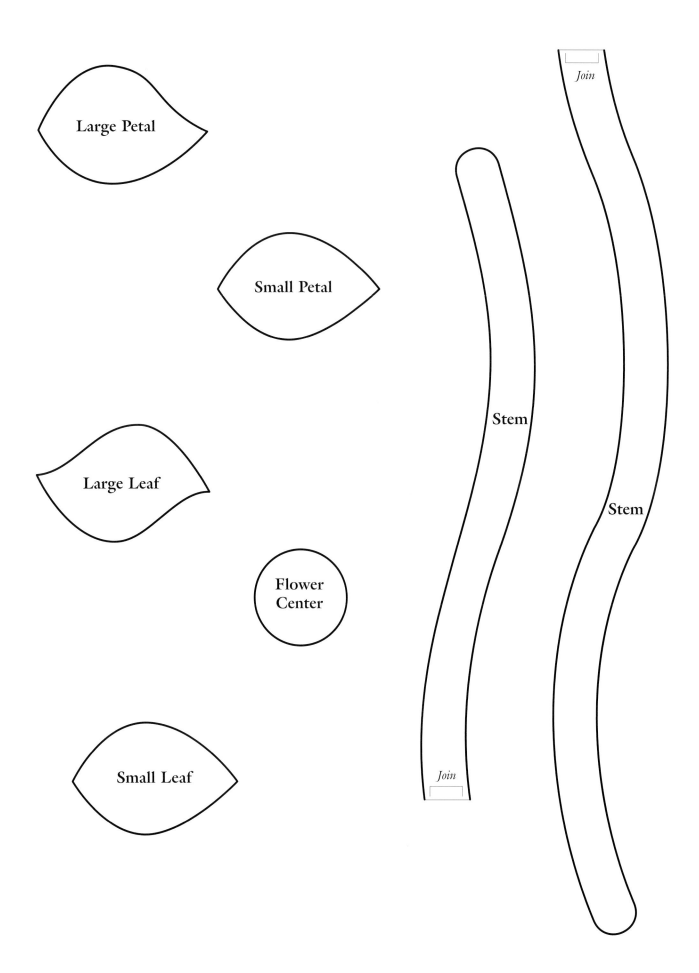

Large Petal

Small Petal

Large Leaf

Flower
Center

Small Leaf

Stem

Stem

Join

Join

Join

Beverly's Mah Jong Mix

1½ cups whole almonds
½ cup sugar
¼ teaspoon cinnamon
2 tablespoons butter

In a heavy, 8-inch skillet, combine all ingredients. Stirring constantly with a wooden spoon, cook over medium to medium-high heat for 6 to 8 minutes or until sugar melts and is golden in color and the nuts are toasted. Spread nuts on greased, foil-lined baking sheets. Cool, then separate into clusters. Serves 6.

Mae's Christmas Posies

Mae never celebrated Christmas until she moved to Happy Valley and then she never stopped. She put her very first Christmas tree up in her living room in 1982 - the year they arrived from Hong Kong, and it has never come down. Of course, it's artificial, just like the wreath on the door and the cat on the davenport. She just couldn't bring herself to take the tree down so she didn't. But she does change the decorations for each holiday - like on Easter she puts eggs on the tree and on Halloween she hangs up little pumpkins – so there really isn't any dust-buildup that you can see. Mae's entire house is decorated in red and green, and making Christmas quilts is her favorite pastime... this one hangs over her mantel – which is just above her artificial fireplace.

"If you quilt you'll never be without friends."
Mae, 1996

Read General Instructions first or just wing it.
—Mae

Quilt Size: 30½" x 30½" (77 x 77 cm)
Block Size: 9" x 9" (23 x 23 cm)

YARDAGE REQUIREMENTS

Yardage is based on 45" (114 cm) wide fabric.
⅞ yd (80 cm) of cream print
⅛ yd (11 cm) of red small print
¼ yd (23 cm) *total* of assorted red prints
1 yd (91 cm) *total* of assorted green prints
1⅛ yds (1 m) for backing
⅝ yd (57 cm) for binding
You will also need:
38" x 38" (97 x 97 cm) square of batting
Template plastic
Green embroidery floss
Water- or air-soluble fabric pen

CUTTING OUT THE PIECES

*Refer to **Template Cutting**, page 85, to make templates for appliqué. Appliqué patterns are on page 68 and do not include seam allowance. Seam allowance should be added for traditional needle-turn appliqué. Follow **Rotary Cutting**, page 82, to cut fabric. Measurements listed include ¼" seam allowances. Borders are cut exact length needed.*

1. From cream print:
    *   Cut 1 strip 10½"w. From this strip, cut **4 large squares** 10½" x 10½".
    *   Cut 2 **top/bottom 4th borders** 1½" x 30".
    *   Cut 2 **side 4th borders** 1½" x 28".
    *   Cut 2 **top/bottom 2nd borders** 3¼" x 26".
    *   Cut 2 **side 2nd borders** 3¼" x 20½".
    *   Cut 16 **posy centers**.

2. From red small print:
    *   Cut 2 **top/bottom 1st borders** 1½" x 20½".
    *   Cut 2 **side 1st borders** 1½" x 18½".
3. From assorted red prints:
    *   Cut 32 **rectangles** 1½" x 2".
    *   Cut 4 **small squares** 1½" x 1½".
    *   Cut 16 **posies**.
4. From assorted green prints:
    *   Cut 36 **rectangles** 1½" x 2".
    *   Cut **bias strip** ¾" x 120", piecing as necessary.
    *   Cut 48 **large leaves**.
    *   Cut 16 **small leaves**.

ASSEMBLING THE QUILT TOP

Follow Piecing, page 85, Pressing, page 86, and Needle-turn Appliqué, page 86, to make quilt top.

1. Using water- or air-soluble fabric pen, draw vertical and horizontal lines through center of **large square** (**Fig. 1**). Using drawn lines as guide for appliqué placement, arrange 4 **posies**, 4 **posy centers**, 4 **large leaves**, and 4 **small leaves** onto **square**; appliqué in place.

Fig. 1

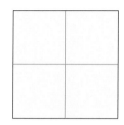

2. Make French Knots between **leaves** and **posies** using 6 strands of green floss. Centering appliquéd design, trim square to 9¹/₂" x 9¹/₂" to make **Appliquéd Block**. Make 4 **Appliquéd Blocks**.

Appliquéd Block (make 4)

3. Sew 2 **Appliquéd Blocks** together to make **Row**. Make 2 **Rows**. Sew **Rows** together to complete center section of quilt top.

4. Alternating green and red, sew 9 green and 8 red **rectangles** together to make **side 3rd border**. Make 2 **side 3rd borders**.

Side 3rd Border (make 2)

5. Alternating green and red, sew 9 green and 8 red **rectangles** together, then sew 1 red **small square** to each end to make **top 3rd border**. Repeat to make **bottom 3rd border**.

Top/Bottom 3rd Border (make 2)

6. Sew **side**, **top**, then **bottom 1st borders** to center section. Repeat to add **2nd**, **3rd**, and **4th borders**.

7. Matching wrong sides, fold **bias strip** in half lengthwise; *do not press*. Stitch along length of strip, ¹/₄" from fold. Trim seam allowance to approximately ¹/₁₆". Centering seam on back of strip, press bias strip flat.

8. Pin or baste bias strip (vine) in place on **second border**; appliqué in place. Arrange 32 **large leaves** around vine; appliqué in place.

COMPLETING THE QUILT

1. Follow **Quilting**, page 88, to mark, layer and quilt as desired. Our quilt is hand quilted. The center section background is crosshatch quilted and the first and fourth borders are outline quilted. The second border is echo quilted around the vine and leaves, and the third border has diagonal lines quilted in the rectangles and small squares.

2. Cut a 20" square of binding fabric. Follow **Binding**, page 92, to bind quilt using 2¹/₂"w bias binding with mitered corners.

Quilt Top Diagram

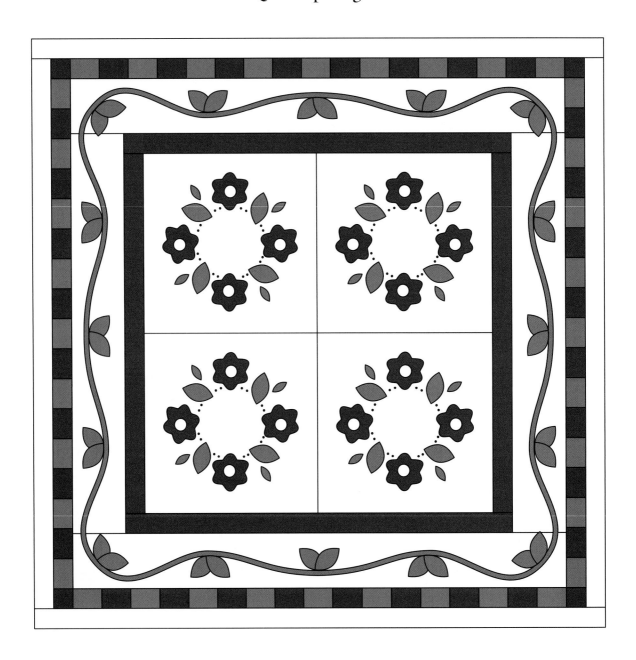

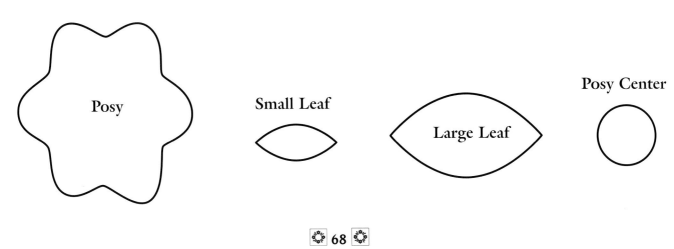

Posy

Small Leaf

Large Leaf

Posy Center

Mae's Hong Kong Lettuce Wraps

ORIENTAL DRESSING

¹/₄ cup peanut oil

3 tablespoons rice vinegar

2 tablespoons soy sauce

2 tablespoons sugar

¹/₄ cup finely chopped parsley

¹/₂ teaspoon black pepper

¹/₄ teaspoon ground ginger

LETTUCE WRAPS

12 skinless, boneless, chicken tenderloins

1¹/₂ tablespoons peanut oil

1 package (6 ounces) rice noodles

1 medium cucumber

2 medium carrots, peeled

¹/₂ cup bean sprouts, fresh or canned

¹/₄ cup sesame seeds, toasted

1 large head leafy lettuce (butter or Romaine lettuce)

Combine dressing ingredients; set aside.

In a medium skillet over medium heat, cook the chicken in peanut oil until done, about 15 to 20 minutes; set aside. Cook rice noodles according to package directions. Rinse and drain; set aside. Slice cucumber into very thin slices; set aside. Grate the carrots; set aside. When the chicken is cool to the touch, slice into thin pieces. Wash and dry lettuce and separate into individual leaves. On a large platter, arrange the cucumber, carrots, bean sprouts, sesame seeds, chicken and lettuce leaves. Place a small bowl of Oriental Dressing in center of platter. Serve by having guests make their own wraps using the lettuce leaf as their wrap, adding all of the ingredients and topping with the dressing. Roll up and enjoy! Serves 8 to 10.

Inga's
Flying Pinwheels

Inga made her Flying Pinwheel quilt to use at the annual Happy Valley Family Day Picnic that is held every July 24th. The whole town dresses up like their ancestors and congregates at the park behind the Grange. The mayor, Inga's husband, is also the leader of the Happy Valley Funeral and Marching Band so while he's acting in his official capacities, Inga sets herself down on her flying pinwheels and watches the "goings on." This little quilt gets lots of attention so Inga is never by herself for long.

"I'm more of a Fabric Manipulator than a quilter."
Inga, 1995

Quilt Size: 57" x 63" (145 x 160 cm)
Block Size: 6" x 6" (15 x 15 cm)

YARDAGE REQUIREMENTS

Yardage is based on 45" (114 cm) wide fabric.

2$^1/_2$ yds (2.3 m) *total* of at least 8 assorted red prints

2$^5/_8$ yds (2.4 m) *total* of at least 8 assorted cream prints

1$^1/_2$ yds (1.4 m) of red and cream stripe

1$^1/_2$ yds (1.4 m) of cream print

4 yds (3.7 m) for backing

$^7/_8$ yd (80 cm) for binding

65" x 71" (165 x 180 cm) piece of batting

Read General Instructions first or have extra fabric and a seam ripper handy!
—*Inga*

CUTTING OUT THE PIECES

*Follow **Rotary Cutting**, page 82, to cut fabric. All measurements include $^1/_4$" seam allowance. Borders are cut exact length needed.*

1. **From assorted red prints:**
   - Cut 112 **large squares** 3$^7/_8$" x 3$^7/_8$".
   - Cut 102 **rectangles** 4$^1/_2$" x 2$^1/_2$".
   - Cut 1 square 5$^1/_4$" x 5$^1/_4$" from *each* of 8 different prints. Cut squares *twice* diagonally to make 32 **triangles**. (You will use only 1 triangle from each square.)

2. **From assorted cream prints:**
   - Cut 112 **large squares** 3$^7/_8$" x 3$^7/_8$".
   - Cut 204 **small squares** 2$^1/_2$" x 2$^1/_2$".
   - Cut 1 square 5$^1/_4$" x 5$^1/_4$" from *each* of 8 different prints. Cut squares *twice* diagonally to make 32 **triangles**. (You will use only 1 **triangle** from each square.)

3. **From red and cream stripe:**
   - Cut 2 *lengthwise* **side 3rd borders** 1$^3/_4$" x 52".
   - Cut 2 *lengthwise* **top/bottom 3rd borders** 1$^3/_4$" x 48$^1/_2$".
   - Cut 2 *lengthwise* **side 1st borders** 1$^3/_4$" x 48$^1/_2$".
   - Cut 2 *lengthwise* **top/bottom 1st borders** 1$^3/_4$" x 45".

4. **From cream print:**
   - Cut 2 *lengthwise* **side 2nd borders** 1" x 51".
   - Cut 2 *lengthwise* **top/bottom 2nd borders** 1" x 46".

ASSEMBLING THE QUILT TOP

Follow Piecing, page 85, and Pressing, page 86, to make quilt top.

1. Draw diagonal line (corner to corner) on wrong side of each cream **large square**. With right sides together, place 1 cream **large square** on top of 1 red **large square**. Stitch seam ¼" from each side of drawn line (**Fig. 1**).

Fig. 1

2. Trim along drawn line and press open to make 2 **triangle-squares**. Make 224 **triangle-squares**.

Triangle-Squares (make 224)

3. Turning **triangle-squares** as shown, sew 4 **triangle-squares** together to make **Pinwheel Block**. Make 56 **Pinwheel Blocks**.

Pinwheel Block (make 56)

4. Referring to **Quilt Top Diagram**, page 74, sew 7 **Pinwheel Blocks** together to make **Row**. Make 8 **Rows**. Sew **Rows** together to complete center section of quilt top.

5. Sew **side**, **top**, then **bottom 1st borders** to center section of quilt top. Repeat to add **2nd** and **3rd borders** to quilt top.

6. Refer to **Flying Geese Diagrams** to make **Flying Geese** for **4th border**. Place 1 **small square** on **rectangle** (right sides together) and stitch diagonal line through **square**. Trim ¼" from stitching line; open and press. Place another **small square** on opposite end of **rectangle**. Stitch as shown and trim; open and press. Make 102 **Flying Geese**.

Flying Geese Diagrams

7. To make **Hourglass Blocks** for **4th border** corners, sew 4 **triangles** together as shown in **Hourglass Block Diagrams**. Make 4 **Hourglass Blocks**.

Hourglass Block Diagrams

8. Sew 27 **Flying Geese** together to make **side 4th border**. Make 2 **side 4th borders**.

9. Sew 24 **Flying Geese** together to make center section of **top 4th border**. Sew **Hourglass Block** to each end to complete **top 4th border**. Repeat to make **bottom 4th border**.

10. Sew **side**, **top**, then **bottom 4th borders** to quilt top.

COMPLETING THE QUILT

1. Follow **Quilting**, page 88, to mark, layer and quilt as desired. Our quilt is machine quilted. The 1st and 3rd borders are outline quilted. The Pinwheel Block section and the red portions of the 4th border are stipple quilted.

2. Cut a 27" square of binding fabric. Follow **Binding**, page 92, to bind quilt using 2^1/$_2$"w bias binding with mitered corners.

Quilt Top Diagram

Inga's **Swedish Meatball Stew**

1 pound ground beef
1 pound ground pork
¹/₂ cup crushed saltine crackers
¹/₂ cup milk
2 eggs, slightly beaten
1 tablespoon finely chopped onion
1 teaspoon salt
1 teaspoon sugar
¹/₄ teaspoon pepper
¹/₂ teaspoon ground allspice
¹/₄ teaspoon ground nutmeg
¹/₄ teaspoon ground ginger
¹/₄ cup butter or margarine
¹/₂ cup plus 4 tablespoons flour, divided
3 cups cream
2 cans (10 ounces each) cream of
 mushroom soup
1 can (10 ounces) beef consommé (not bouillon)
salt and pepper to taste
2 large carrots, peeled and sliced

2 large potatoes, peeled and diced into
 1-inch cubes
¹/₄ cup chopped onion
1 stalk celery, chopped

Combine ground beef and pork with saltines, ¹/₂ cup milk, eggs, finely chopped onion and seasonings. Shape into 24 large meatballs (approximately 2 inches in diameter). Melt butter or margarine in a large skillet. Roll meatballs in ¹/₂ cup flour and place in skillet over medium-high heat to brown, turning constantly so they brown evenly. Cover pan tightly, reduce heat and cook about 15 to 20 minutes or until meatballs are cooked thoroughly. Remove meatballs from skillet and place in a 4-quart casserole; set aside. In the same skillet, add 4 tablespoons flour and mix with drippings in the pan. Stirring constantly, add cream, mushroom soup and consommé; blend well. Season mixture with salt and pepper. Add carrots, potatoes, onion and celery to meatballs. Pour soup mixture over meatballs and bake in oven for 2 hours at 350 degrees. Serves 8.

Ginny's Red and White

Ginny made this quilt out of fabric she inherited from her Great Aunt Edna. Aunt Edna was the Queen of UFO's and had bags and bags of projects stashed around her house. Ginny knew some of these projects might be passed her way and as one of the "favorite nieces" she thought she might inherit Great Aunt Edna's stamp collection– it was worth thousands and thousands of dollars. But what she most hoped to get from Great Aunt Edna (for the funeral home) was the 3 albums of celebrity obituaries that Edna (and her mother) had cut and pasted for nearly 100 years. Every famous person who had died between 1900 and 1995 was in those books – now that would have been a real prize but it went to her cousin, Turk, who laid claim to them because he is in show business himself – he runs the Happy Valley theater. So while Ginny missed out on the celebrity obits, she did inherit 17 bags of fabric from Great Aunt Edna (and the Stamp Collection!) and inside one of those bags was the fabric for this quilt. All things considered, not a bad inheritance!

"The one who dies with the most UFO's
(UnFinished Objects) better be leaving something to me!"
Ginny, 1993

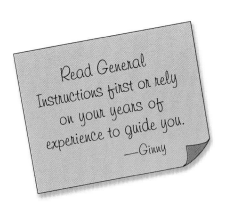

Read General Instructions first or rely on your years of experience to guide you.
—Ginny

Quilt Size: 76 " x 76" (193 x 193 cm)

YARDAGE REQUIREMENTS

Yardage is based on 45" (114 cm) wide fabric.
$3^{1}/_{2}$ yds (3.2 m) of red solid
$3^{1}/_{2}$ yds (3.2 m) of white solid
$4^{3}/_{4}$ yds (4.3 m) for backing
$^{7}/_{8}$ yd (80 cm) for binding
You will also need:
84" x 84" (213 x 213 cm) square of batting
Template plastic

CUTTING OUT THE PIECES

*Follow **Template Cutting**, page 85, to cut template from **pattern A** on page 80.*

1. **From red solid:**
   • Cut 157 **A's** from template.
2. **From white solid:**
   • Cut 158 **A's** from template.

ASSEMBLING THE QUILT TOP

*Follow **Piecing**, page 85, and **Pressing**, page 86, to make quilt top. Use $^{1}/_{4}$" seam allowances throughout.*

1. Matching dots, sew 1 white solid **A** and 1 red solid **A** together as shown in **Fig. 1**. Alternating colors, sew a total of 8 white solid **A's** and 7 red solid **A's** together to make vertical **Row A**. Make 11 **Row A's**.

Fig. 1

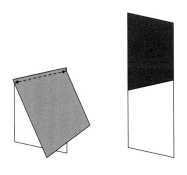

2. Matching dots and alternating colors, sew 8 red solid **A's** and 7 white solid **A's** together to make vertical **Row B**. Make 10 **Row B's**.
3. Alternating **Row A's** and **Row B's**, sew **Rows** together to complete quilt top.
4. Trim top and bottom of quilt top even with inner points (**Fig. 2**).

Fig. 2

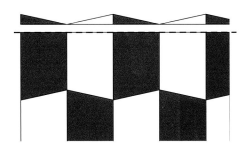

COMPLETING THE QUILT

1. Follow **Quilting**, page 88, to mark, layer and quilt as desired. Our quilt is machine quilted with a meandering star pattern using red thread.
2. Cut a 30" square of binding fabric. Follow **Binding**, page 92, to bind quilt using $2^{1}/_{2}$"w bias binding with mitered corners.

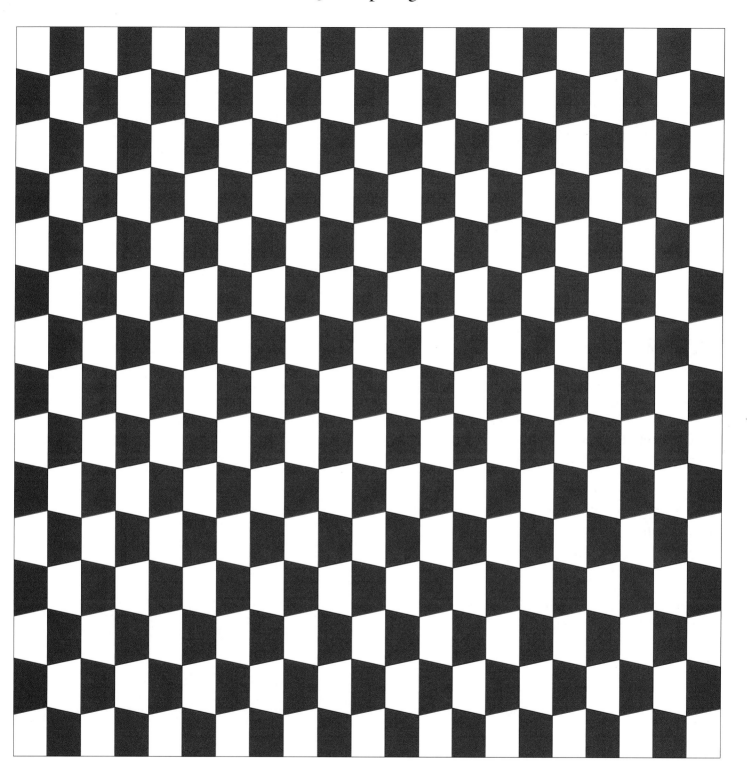

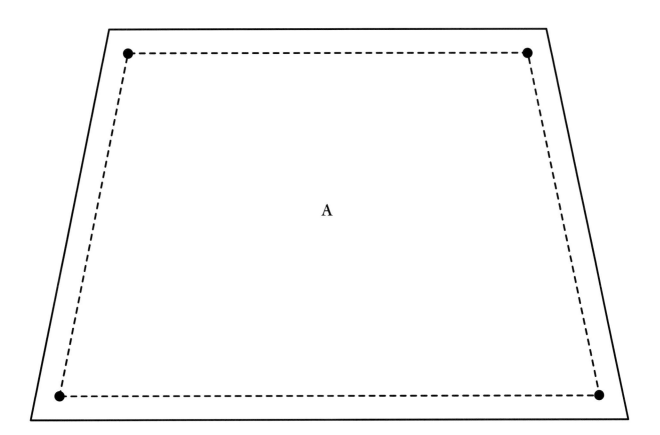

A

GINNY'S ODE TO UFO'S
(UnFinished Objects)

They lurk in baskets, on shelves and
in drawers,
In closets, under beds, behind
bedroom doors.
They taunt me and tease me and fill
me with guilt
For the hours of time and the money
I've spilt!

I try not to think about them, try not
to see,
All the mistakes that were made by
little 'ol me!
Those darned UFO's, what's a quilter
to do?
Finish them? Well, what have I got
to lose?

I'll lose the bags filled with pieces too
many to count!

I'll lose the baskets with fabrics
stacked like a mount!
I'll lose the guilt that I save for my
weekly sew day!
And maybe I'll lose "procrastination"
along the way!

Oh, UFO's, show me where to start!
I'm ready to begin tearing you apart.
I'll work on you slowly, day after day,
Until you are done and out of
my way!

You won't hold me hostage any
longer dear UFO
Because once you are finished I know
where you'll go!
Over the mantel, on the railing, or on
top of my bed
Where I can see you each day as pride
fills my head!

Ginny's **Funeral Potatoes**

Also great for happier occasions like bridal or baby showers.

CASEROLE

> 1 package (32 ounces) frozen hash brown
>   potatoes
> 2 cans (10³/₄ ounces each) cream of chicken soup
> 2 cups sour cream
> ¹/₂ cup melted margarine or butter
> ¹/₂ cup chopped onion
> 1 teaspoon salt
> ¹/₄ teaspoon black pepper
> 2 cups shredded Cheddar cheese

TOPPING

> 4 cups crushed corn flakes
> ¹/₂ cup melted margarine or butter

Thaw potatoes. Combine soup, sour cream, melted margarine, onion, salt, pepper and cheese. Blend with potatoes and pour into a 9 x 13-inch baking pan.

Combine topping ingredients. Sprinkle topping over potatoes. Bake for 45 minutes at 350 degrees. Cover with foil, if necessary, to prevent excessive browning. Serves 8 to 10 bereaved.

General Instructions

To make your quilting easier and more enjoyable, we encourage you to carefully read all of the general instructions, study the color photographs, and familiarize yourself with the individual project instructions before beginning a project.

FABRICS

SELECTING FABRICS

Choose high-quality, medium-weight 100% cotton fabrics. All-cotton fabrics hold a crease better, fray less, and are easier to quilt than cotton/polyester blends.

Yardage requirements listed for each project are based on 45" wide fabric with a "usable" width of 42" after shrinkage and trimming selvages. Actual usable width will probably vary slightly from fabric to fabric. Our recommended yardage lengths should be adequate for occasional resquaring of fabric when many cuts are required. Cut pieces from each fabric in the order listed in project cutting instructions.

PREPARING FABRICS

We recommend that all fabrics be washed, dried, and pressed before cutting. If fabrics are not pre-washed, washing finished quilt will cause shrinkage and give it a more "antiqued" look and feel. Bright and dark colors, which may run, should always be washed before cutting. After washing and drying fabric, fold lengthwise with wrong sides together and matching selvages.

ROTARY CUTTING

*Based on the idea that you can easily cut strips of fabric and then cut those strips into smaller pieces, rotary cutting has brought speed and accuracy to quiltmaking. Observe safety precautions when using the rotary cutter, since it is extremely sharp. Develop a habit of retracting the blade guard **just before** making a cut and closing it **immediately afterward**, before laying down the cutter.*

1. Cut all strips from the selvage-to-selvage width of the fabric unless otherwise indicated in project instructions. Place fabric on the cutting mat, as shown in **Fig. 1**, with the fold of the fabric toward you. To straighten the uneven fabric edge, make the first "squaring up" cut by placing the right edge of the rotary cutting ruler over the left raw edge of the fabric. Place right-angle triangle (or another rotary cutting ruler) with the lower edge carefully aligned with the fold and the left edge against the ruler (**Fig. 1**). Hold the ruler firmly with your left hand, placing your little finger off the left edge to anchor the ruler. Remove the triangle, pick up the rotary cutter, and retract the blade guard. Using a smooth downward motion, make the cut by running the blade of the rotary cutter firmly along the right edge of the ruler (**Fig. 2**). **Always** cut in a direction away from your body and **immediately** close the blade guard after each cut.

Fig. 1

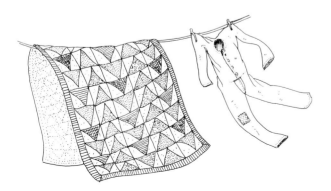

Fig. 2

2. To cut each of the strips required for a project, place the ruler over the cut edge of the fabric, aligning desired marking on the ruler with the cut edge (**Fig. 3**); make the cut. When cutting several strips from a single piece of fabric, it is important to occasionally use the ruler and triangle to ensure that cuts are still at a perfect right angle to the fold. If not, repeat Step 1 to straighten.

Fig. 3

3. To square up selvage ends of a strip before cutting pieces, refer to **Fig. 4** and place folded strip on mat with selvage ends to your right. Aligning a horizontal marking on ruler with 1 long edge of strip, use rotary cutter to trim selvage to make end of strip square and even (**Fig. 4**). Turn strip (or entire mat) so that cut end is to your left before making subsequent cuts.

Fig. 4

4. Pieces such as rectangles and squares can now be cut from strips. Usually strips remain folded, and pieces are cut in pairs after ends of strips are squared up. To cut squares or rectangles from a strip, place ruler over left end of strip, aligning desired marking on ruler with cut end of strip. To ensure perfectly square cuts, align a horizontal marking on ruler with 1 long edge of strip (**Fig. 5**) before making the cut.

Fig. 5

5. To cut 2 triangles from a square, cut square the size indicated in the project instructions. Cut square once diagonally to make 2 triangles (**Fig. 6**).

Fig. 6

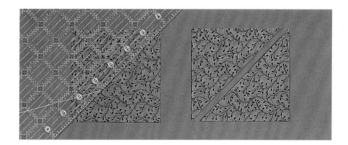

6. To cut 4 triangles from a square, cut square the size indicated in the project instructions. Cut square twice diagonally to make 4 triangles (**Fig. 7**). You may find it helpful to use a small rotary cutting mat so that the mat can be turned to make second cut without disturbing fabric pieces.

Fig. 7

7. After some practice, you may want to try stacking up to 6 fabric layers when making cuts. When stacking strips, match long cut edges and follow Step 3 to square up ends of strip stack. Carefully turn stack (or entire mat) so that squared-up ends are to your left before making subsequent cuts. After cutting, check accuracy of pieces. Some shapes, such as diamonds, are more difficult to cut accurately in stacks.

8. In some cases, strips will be sewn together into strip sets before being cut into smaller units. When cutting a strip set, align a seam in strip set with a horizontal marking on the ruler to maintain square cuts (**Fig. 8**). We do not recommend stacking strip sets for rotary cutting.

Fig. 8

9. Some borders for quilts in this book are cut along the more stable lengthwise grain to minimize wavy edges caused by stretching. To remove selvages before cutting lengthwise strips, place fabric on mat with selvages to your left and squared-up end at bottom of mat. Placing ruler over selvage and using squared-up edge instead of fold, follow Step 2 to cut away selvages as you did raw edges (**Fig. 9**). After making a cut the length of the mat, move the next section of fabric to be cut onto the mat. Repeat until you have removed selvages from required length of fabric.

Fig. 9

10. After removing selvages, place ruler over left edge of fabric, aligning desired marking on ruler with cut edge of fabric. Make cuts as in Step 2. After each cut, move next section of fabric onto mat as in Step 9.

Tip from Alice

Always use a rotary cutter with a sharp blade - but don't throw your old blades out. Save them and use two at a time in your cutter if you run out of new blades - chances are they won't have nicks or wear in the same spot so you'll be cutting smoothly again in no time.

TEMPLATE CUTTING

Our piecing template patterns have 2 lines – a solid cutting line and a dashed line showing the ¹/4" seam allowance. (Patterns for appliqué templates do not include seam allowances.)

1. To make a template from a pattern, use a permanent fine-point pen to carefully trace pattern onto template plastic, making sure to transfer any alignment markings. Cut out template along inner edge of drawn line. Check template against original pattern for accuracy.

2. Place template face down on wrong side of fabric (unless otherwise indicated in project instructions), aligning grain line on template with straight grain of fabric. Use a sharp fabric-marking pencil to draw around template. Transfer all alignment markings to fabric. Cut out fabric piece using scissors or rotary cutting equipment.

Tip from Alice

Make your scissors easier to cut with by rubbing them with a fabric softener dryer sheet. Also, make sure you have at least 3 pairs of scissors: one for the kids, one for paper, and one just for your fabric!

PIECING

Precise cutting, followed by accurate piecing, will ensure that all pieces of quilt top fit together well.

HAND PIECING

- Use ruler and sharp fabric marking pencil to draw all seam lines and transfer any alignment markings onto back of cut pieces.

- Matching right sides, pin 2 pieces together, using pins to mark corners.

- Use Running Stitch to sew pieces together along drawn line, backstitching at beginning and end of seam.

- Run 5 or 6 stitches onto needle before pulling needle through fabric.

- To add stability, backstitch every ³/4" to 1".

- Do not extend stitches into seam allowances.

MACHINE PIECING

- Set sewing machine stitch length for approximately 11 stitches per inch.

- Use neutral-colored general-purpose sewing thread (not quilting thread) in needle and in bobbin.

- An accurate ¹/4" seam allowance is *essential*. Presser feet that are ¹/4" wide are available for most sewing machines.

- When piecing, always place pieces right sides together and match raw edges; pin if necessary.

- Chain piecing saves time and will usually result in more accurate piecing.

- Trim away points of seam allowances that extend beyond edges of sewn pieces.

Sewing Strip Sets

When there are several strips to assemble into a strip set, first sew strips together into pairs, then sew pairs together to form strip set. To help avoid distortion, sew seams in opposite directions (**Fig. 10**).

Fig. 10

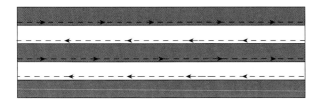

Sewing Across Seam Intersections

When sewing across intersection of 2 seams, place pieces right sides together and match seams exactly, making sure seam allowances are pressed in opposite directions (**Fig. 11**).

Fig. 11

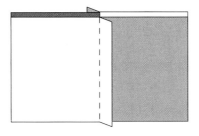

Sewing Sharp Points

To ensure sharp points when joining triangular or diagonal pieces, stitch across the center of the "X" (shown in pink) formed on wrong side by previous seams (**Fig. 12**).

Fig. 12

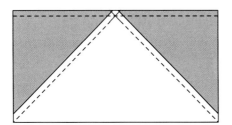

PRESSING

- Use steam iron set on "Cotton" for all pressing.

- Press after sewing each seam.

- Seam allowances are almost always pressed to 1 side, usually toward darker fabric. However, to reduce bulk it may occasionally be necessary to press seam allowances toward the lighter fabric or even to press them open.

- To prevent dark fabric seam allowance from showing through light fabric, trim darker seam allowance slightly narrower than lighter seam allowance.

- To press long seams, such as those in long strip sets, without curving or other distortion, lay strips across width of the ironing board.

NEEDLE-TURN APPLIQUÉ

Using needle to turn under seam allowance while blindstitching appliqué to background fabric is called "needle-turn appliqué."

1. Place template on right side of appliqué fabric. Lightly draw around template with pencil, leaving at least $1/2$" between shapes. Repeat for number of shapes specified in project instructions.
2. Cut out shapes approximately $3/16$" outside drawn line. Clip curves up to, but not through, drawn line. Arrange shapes on background fabric and pin or baste in place.
3. Thread a sharps needle with a single strand of general-purpose sewing thread that matches appliqué; knot one end.

4. Begin blindstitching on as straight an edge as possible, turning a small section of seam allowance to wrong side with needle, concealing drawn line (**Fig. 13**).

Fig. 13

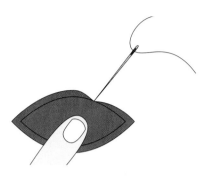

5. To stitch outward points, stitch to $\frac{1}{2}$" from point (**Fig. 14**). Turn seam allowance under at point (**Fig. 15**); then turn remainder of seam allowance between stitching and point. Stitch to point, taking 2 or 3 stitches at top of point to secure. Turn under small amount of seam allowance past point and resume stitching.

Fig. 14

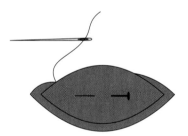

Fig. 15

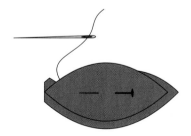

6. To stitch inward point, stitch to $\frac{1}{2}$" from point (**Fig. 16**). Clip to, but not through, drawn line at point (**Fig. 17**). Turn seam allowance under between stitching and point. Stitch to point, taking 2 or 3 stitches at point to secure. Turn under small amount of seam allowance past point and resume stitching.

Fig. 16

Fig. 17

7. Do not turn under or stitch seam allowances that will be covered by other appliqué pieces.
8. To appliqué pressed bias strips, baste strips in place and blindstitch along edges.
9. To reduce bulk, background fabric behind appliqués may be cut away. After stitching appliqués in place, turn block over and use sharp scissors or specially designed appliqué scissors to trim away background fabric approximately $\frac{3}{16}$" from stitching line. Take care not to cut appliqué fabric or stitches.

QUILTING

Quilting holds the 3 layers (top, batting, and backing) of the quilt together and can be done by hand or machine. Because marking, layering, and quilting are interrelated and may be done in different orders depending on circumstances, please read entire Quilting *section before beginning project.*

TYPES OF QUILTING DESIGNS

In the Ditch Quilting
Quilting along seamlines or along edges of appliquéd pieces is called "in the ditch" quilting. This type of quilting should be done on side **opposite** seam allowance and does not have to be marked.

Outline Quilting
Quilting a consistent distance, usually $^{1}/_{4}$", from seam or appliqué is called "outline" quilting. Outline quilting may be marked, or $^{1}/_{4}$" masking tape may be placed along seamlines for quilting guide. (Do not leave tape on quilt longer than necessary, since it may leave an adhesive residue.)

Motif Quilting
Quilting a design, such as a feathered wreath, is called "motif" quilting. This type of quilting should be marked before basting quilt layers together.

Echo Quilting
Quilting that follows the outline of an appliquéd or pieced design with 2 or more parallel lines is called "echo" quilting. This type of quilting does not need to be marked.

Channel Quilting
Quilting with straight, parallel lines is called "channel" quilting. This type of quilting may be marked or stitched using a guide.

Crosshatch Quilting
Quilting straight lines in a grid pattern is called "crosshatch" quilting. Lines may be stitched parallel to edges of quilt or stitched diagonally. This type of quilting may be marked or stitched using a guide.

Meandering Quilting
Quilting in random curved lines and swirls is called "meandering" quilting. Quilting lines should not cross or touch each other. This type of quilting does not need to be marked.

Stipple Quilting
Meandering quilting that is very closely spaced is called "stipple" quilting. Stippling will flatten the area quilted and is often stitched in background areas to raise appliquéd or pieced designs. This type of quilting does not need to be marked.

MARKING QUILTING LINES
Quilting lines may be marked using fabric marking pencils, chalk markers, water- or air-soluble pens, or lead pencils.

Simple quilting designs may be marked with chalk or chalk pencil after basting. A small area may be marked, then quilted, before moving to next area to be marked. Intricate designs should be marked before basting using a more durable marker.

Caution: Some marks may be permanently set by pressing. **Test** different markers **on scrap fabric** to find one that marks clearly and can be thoroughly removed.

Tip from Alice

Freeze slivers of soap and use them to mark designs on dark fabrics.

A wide variety of precut quilting stencils, as well as entire books of quilting patterns, are available. Using a stencil makes it easier to mark intricate or repetitive designs.

To make a stencil from a pattern, center template plastic over pattern and use a permanent marker to trace pattern onto plastic. Use a craft knife with single or double blade to cut channels along traced lines (**Fig. 18**).

Fig. 18

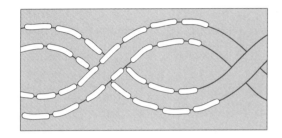

PREPARING THE BACKING

To allow for slight shifting of quilt top during quilting, backing should be approximately 4" larger on all sides. Yardage requirements listed for quilt backings are calculated for 45"w fabric. Using 90"w or 108"w fabric for the backing may eliminate piecing. To piece a backing using 45"w fabric, use the following instructions.

1. Measure length and width of quilt top; add 8" to each measurement.
2. If determined width is 84" or less, cut backing fabric into 2 lengths the determined **length** measurement. Trim selvages. Place lengths with right sides facing and sew long edges together, forming tube (**Fig. 19**). Match seams and press along 1 fold (**Fig. 20**). Cut along pressed fold to form single piece (**Fig. 21**).

Fig. 19   **Fig. 20**   **Fig. 21**

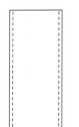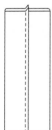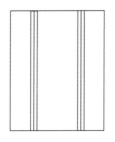

3. If determined width is more than 84", cut backing fabric into 3 lengths the determined **width** measurement. Trim selvages. Sew long edges together to form single piece.
4. Trim backing to size determined in Step 1; press seam allowances open.

CHOOSING THE BATTING

The appropriate batting will make quilting easier. For fine hand quilting, choose low-loft batting. All cotton or cotton/polyester blend battings work well for machine quilting because the cotton helps "grip" quilt layers. If quilt is to be tied, a high-loft batting, sometimes called extra-loft or fat batting, may be used to make quilt "fluffy."

Types of batting include cotton, polyester, cotton/polyester blend, wool, cotton/wool blend, and silk.

When selecting batting, refer to package labels for characteristics and care instructions. Cut batting same size as prepared backing.

ASSEMBLING THE QUILT

1. Examine wrong side of quilt top closely; trim any seam allowances and clip any threads that may show through front of the quilt. Press quilt top, being careful not to "set" any marked quilting lines.
2. Place backing **wrong** side up on flat surface. Use masking tape to tape edges of backing to surface. Place batting on top of backing fabric. Smooth batting gently, being careful not to stretch or tear. Center quilt top **right** side up on batting.

3. If hand quilting, begin in center and work toward outer edges to hand baste all layers together. Use long stitches and place basting lines approximately 4" apart (**Fig. 22**). Smooth fullness or wrinkles toward outer edges.

Fig. 22

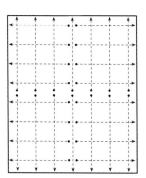

4. If machine quilting, use 1" rustproof safety pins to "pin-baste" all layers together, spacing pins approximately 4" apart. Begin at center and work toward outer edges to secure all layers. If possible, place pins away from areas that will be quilted, although pins may be removed as needed when quilting.

HAND QUILTING

The quilting stitch is a basic running stitch that forms a broken line on quilt top and backing. Stitches on quilt top and backing should be straight and equal in length.

1. Secure center of quilt in hoop or frame. Check quilt top and backing to make sure they are smooth. To help prevent puckers, always begin quilting in the center of quilt and work toward outside edges.

2. Thread needle with 18" - 20" length of quilting thread; knot 1 end. Using thimble, insert needle into quilt top and batting approximately ¹/₂" from quilting line. Bring needle up on quilting line (**Fig. 23**); when knot catches on quilt top, give thread a quick, short pull to "pop" knot through fabric into batting (**Fig. 24**).

Fig. 23   **Fig. 24**

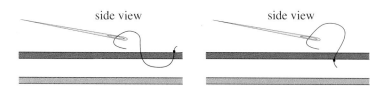

3. Holding needle with sewing hand and placing other hand underneath quilt, use thimble to push tip of needle down through all layers. As soon as needle touches finger underneath, use that finger to push tip of needle only back up through layers to top of quilt. (The amount of needle showing above fabric determines length of quilting stitch.) Referring to **Fig. 25**, rock needle up and down, taking 3 - 6 stitches before bringing needle and thread completely through layers. Check back of quilt to make sure stitches are going through all layers. If necessary, make 1 stitch at a time when quilting through seam allowances or along curves and corners.

Fig. 25

4. At end of thread, knot thread close to fabric and "pop" knot into batting; clip thread close to fabric.

5. Move hoop as often as necessary. Thread may be left dangling and picked up again after returning to that part of quilt.

MACHINE QUILTING METHODS

Use general-purpose thread in bobbin. Do not use quilting thread. Thread the needle of machine with general-purpose thread or transparent monofilament thread to make quilting blend with quilt top fabrics. Use decorative thread, such as a metallic or contrasting-color general-purpose thread, to make quilting lines stand out more.

Straight Line Quilting

The term "straight-line" is somewhat deceptive, since curves (especially gentle ones) as well as straight lines can be stitched with this technique.

1. Set stitch length for 6 - 10 stitches per inch and attach walking foot to sewing machine.

2. Determine which section of quilt will have longest continuous quilting line, oftentimes area from center top to center bottom. Roll up and secure each edge of quilt to help reduce the bulk, keeping fabrics smooth. Smaller projects may not need to be rolled.

3. Begin stitching on longest quilting line, using very short stitches for the first 1/4" to "lock" quilting. Stitch across project, using 1 hand on each side of walking foot to slightly spread fabric and to guide fabric through machine. Lock stitches at end of quilting line.

4. Continue machine quilting, stitching longer quilting lines first to stabilize quilt before moving on to other areas.

Free Motion Quilting

Free motion quilting may be free form or may follow a marked pattern.

1. Attach darning foot to sewing machine and lower or cover feed dogs.

2. Position quilt under darning foot. Holding top thread, take 1 stitch and pull bobbin thread to top of quilt. To "lock" beginning of quilting line, hold top and bobbin threads while making 3 to 5 stitches in place.

3. Use 1 hand on each side of darning foot to slightly spread fabric and to move fabric through the machine. Even stitch length is achieved by using smooth, flowing hand motion and steady machine speed. Slow machine speed and fast hand movement will create long stitches. Fast machine speed and slow hand movement will create short stitches. Move quilt sideways, back and forth, in a circular motion, or in a random motion to create desired designs; do not rotate quilt. Lock stitches at end of each quilting line.

Tip from Alice

Machine quilting can be a pain in the neck - literally - so make sure you're seated higher than your machine to help ease the strain on your neck and shoulders.

MAKING A HANGING SLEEVE

Attaching a hanging sleeve to back of wall hanging or quilt before the binding is added allows project to be displayed on wall.

1. Measure width of quilt top edge and subtract 1". Cut piece of fabric 7"w by determined measurement.
2. Press short edges of fabric piece $1/4$" to wrong side; press edges $1/4$" to wrong side again and machine stitch in place.
3. Matching wrong sides, fold piece in half lengthwise to form tube.
4. Follow project instructions to sew binding to quilt top and to trim backing and batting. Before blindstitching binding to backing, match raw edges and stitch hanging sleeve to center top edge on back of quilt.
5. Finish binding quilt, treating hanging sleeve as part of backing.
6. Blindstitch bottom of hanging sleeve to backing, taking care not to stitch through to front of quilt.

BINDING

Binding encloses the raw edges of quilt. Because of its stretchiness, bias binding works well for binding projects with curves or rounded corners and tends to lie smooth and flat in any given circumstance. Binding may also be cut from straight lengthwise or crosswise grain of fabric.

MAKING CONTINUOUS BIAS STRIP BINDING

Bias strips for binding can simply be cut and pieced to desired length. However, when a long length of binding is needed, the "continuous" method is quick and accurate.

1. Cut square from binding fabric the size indicated in project instructions. Cut square in half diagonally to make 2 triangles.
2. With right sides together and using $1/4$" seam allowance, sew triangles together (**Fig. 26**); press seam allowance open.

Fig. 26

3. On wrong side of fabric, draw lines the width of binding as specified in project instructions, usually $2^1/2$" (**Fig. 27**). Cut off any remaining fabric less than this width.

Fig. 27

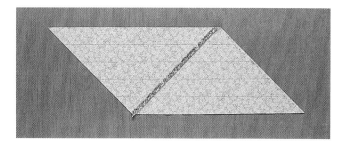

4. With right sides inside, bring short edges together to form tube; match raw edges so that first drawn line of top section meets second drawn line of bottom section (**Fig. 28**).

Fig. 28

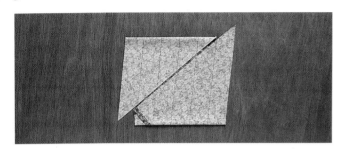

5. Carefully pin edges together by inserting pins through drawn lines at point where drawn lines intersect, making sure pins go through intersections on both sides. Using $^1/_4$" seam allowance, sew edges together; press seam allowance open.
6. To cut continuous strip, begin cutting along first drawn line (**Fig. 29**). Continue cutting along drawn line around tube.

Fig. 29

7. Trim ends of bias strip square.
8. Matching wrong sides and raw edges, press bias strip in half lengthwise to complete binding.

ATTACHING BINDING WITH MITERED CORNERS

1. Press 1 end of binding diagonally (**Fig. 30**).

Fig. 30

2. Beginning with pressed end several inches from a corner, lay binding around quilt to make sure that seams in binding will not end up at a corner. Adjust placement if necessary. Matching raw edges of binding to raw edge of quilt top, pin binding to right side of quilt along 1 edge.
3. When you reach the first corner, mark $^1/_4$" from corner of quilt top (**Fig. 31**).

Fig. 31

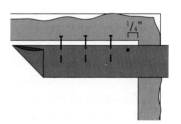

4. Using a ¼" seam allowance, sew binding to quilt, backstitching at beginning of stitching and when you reach the mark (**Fig. 32**). Lift needle out of fabric and clip thread.

Fig. 32

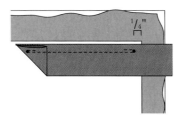

5. Fold binding as shown in **Figs. 33** and **34** and pin binding to adjacent side, matching raw edges. When you reach the next corner, mark ¼" from edge of quilt top.

Fig. 33   **Fig. 34**

   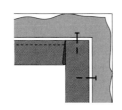

6. Backstitching at edge of quilt top, sew pinned binding to quilt (**Fig. 35**); backstitch when you reach the next mark. Lift needle out of fabric and clip thread.

Fig. 35

7. Repeat Steps 5 and 6 to continue sewing binding to quilt until binding overlaps beginning end by approximately 2". Trim excess binding.

8. If using 2½"w binding (finished size ½"), trim backing and batting a scant ¼" larger than quilt top so that batting and backing will fill the binding when it is folded over to the quilt backing. If using narrower binding, trim backing and batting even with edges of quilt top.

9. On 1 edge of quilt, fold binding over to quilt backing and pin pressed edge in place, covering stitching line (**Fig. 36**). On adjacent side, fold binding over, forming a mitered corner (**Fig. 37**). Repeat to pin remainder of binding in place.

Fig. 36

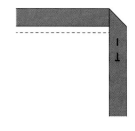

Fig. 37

10. Blindstitch binding to backing, taking care not to stitch through to front of quilt.

SIGNING AND DATING YOUR QUILT

A completed quilt is a work of art and should be signed and dated. There are many different ways to do this and numerous books on the subject. The label should reflect the style of the quilt, the occasion or person for which it was made, and the quilter's own particular talents. Following are suggestions for recording the history of the quilt or adding a sentiment for future generations.

- Embroider quilter's name, date, and any additional information on quilt top or backing. Matching floss, such as cream floss on a white border, will leave a subtle record. Bright or contrasting floss will make the information stand out.
- Make label from muslin and use permanent marker to write information. Use different colored permanent markers to make label more decorative. Stitch label to back of quilt.
- Use photo-transfer paper to add image to white or cream fabric label. Stitch label to back of quilt.
- Piece an extra block from quilt top pattern to use as label. Add information with permanent fabric pen. Appliqué block to back of quilt.
- Write message on appliquéd design from quilt top. Attach appliqué to back of the quilt.

HAND STITCHES
BLIND STITCH

Come up at 1, go down at 2, and come up at 3 (**Fig. 38**). Length of stitches may be varied as desired.

Fig. 38

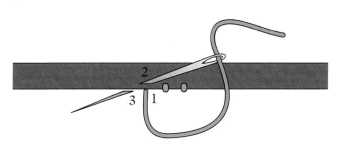

FRENCH KNOT

Follow **Figs. 39 – 42** to complete French Knots. Come up at 1. Wrap thread twice around needle and insert needle at 2, holding end of thread with non-stitching fingers. Tighten knot then pull needle through, holding floss until it must be released.

Fig. 39 **Fig. 40**

 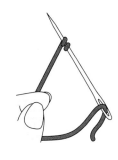

Fig. 41 **Fig. 42**

Metric Conversion Chart	
Inches x 2.54 = centimeters (cm)	Yards x .9144 = meters (m)
Inches x 25.4 = millimeters (mm)	Yards x 91.44 = centimeters (cm)
Inches x .0254 = meters (m)	Centimeters x .3937 = inches (")
	Meters x 1.0936 = yards (yd)

Standard Equivalents					
1/8"	3.2 mm	0.32 cm	1/8 yard	11.43 cm	0.11 m
1/4"	6.35 mm	0.635 cm	1/4 yard	22.86 cm	0.23 m
3/8"	9.5 mm	0.95 cm	3/8 yard	34.29 cm	0.34 m
1/2"	12.7 mm	1.27 cm	1/2 yard	45.72 cm	0.46 m
5/8"	15.9 mm	1.59 cm	5/8 yard	57.15 cm	0.57 m
3/4"	19.1 mm	1.91 cm	3/4 yard	68.58 cm	0.69 m
7/8"	22.2 mm	2.22 cm	7/8 yard	80 cm	0.8 m
1"	25.4 mm	2.54 cm	1 yard	91.44 cm	0.91 m